Sounds of Singing Teacher's Book
Y3-4/P4-5

Alison Ley

Published in 2003 by:
Nelson Thornes Ltd
Delta Place
27 Bath Road
CHELTENHAM
GL53 7TH
United Kingdom

02 03 04 05 06 / 10 9 8 7 6 5 4 3 2 1

A catalogue record for this book is available from the British Library

ISBN 0 17 427099 2

Music notation by Linda Lancaster Music Setting, Huddersfield
Page make-up by Florence Production Limited, Stoodleigh, Devon

Printed in Croatia by Zrinski

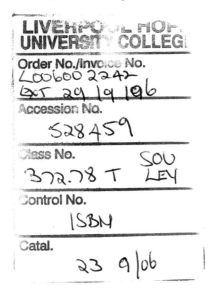

Contents

Foreword

These are interesting times for singing, and particularly for singing in school. Challenged by exciting advances in instrumental music and latterly in music technology, and sidelined by popular musical culture, 'choral' singing has over the last half-century lost its natural place at the centre of children's musical experience.

Boys in particular are reluctant to sing, for complex sociological and cultural reasons. At the same time our innate tribal need to communicate through song is there as much as ever, as evidenced from the football field to the opera house.

The good news is that we have a change in the tide. It was a joy for me to be a member of the working group which created the first National Curriculum for music back in 1991, and which provided the chance to state clearly the place of singing at the core of musical activity and of learning. There is right now a unique opportunity to develop new ways to exploit our most economical natural musical resource, the singing voice.

The biggest single issue now is helping teachers to deliver. There is an urgent need to help build their confidence and skills, by providing user-friendly source materials and schemes of work. Here we have a splendid answer.

Sounds of Singing works in the best sense from the ground upwards.

The secret is lateral thinking – new strategies to subvert the reluctance of pupils to come out of hiding and express themselves vocally, and to develop their singing skills step by step, alongside their enjoyment in working through appealingly presented material.

Each lesson introduces an aspect of singing technique, a new musical style, the opportunity to improvise and create sounds and to develop musicianship and memory. Listening and performing go side by side here, and the activities and their outcomes are presented in a way which even the most inexperienced teacher will find supportive and non-threatening.

The use of CD performances of pieces is a masterstroke, and the performances are of a high quality too. Backing tracks are separated from the vocals, offering a variety of learning methods.

All in all, *Sounds of Singing* is a magnificent concept, and an invaluable resource for all primary music teachers. With materials like this, we can take the tide at the flood, and get surfing.

Mike Brewer OBE
Musical Director, National Youth Choirs
of Great Britain and Laudibus

All about Sounds of Singing

The task ahead

The voice is the one musical instrument that we all possess. It is portable, requires little maintenance and is a great means of expression. In an ideal world, teachers would sing happily and uninhibitedly with their children (and some do), but many of us do not find this very easy. The whole process involves both teacher and pupil in physical skills, memory skills, listening skills, language skills and vocal skills. Learning songs to practise all these skills can only be pleasurable if the materials used are reassuringly accessible and stimulating, are carefully graded, come in bite size portions and give clear guidance on how to get the very best out of every song. Above all the whole process must be made enjoyable. *Sounds of Singing* provides all this.

Who can use *Sounds of Singing*?

Sounds of Singing is for both the musically experienced and musically inexperienced primary classroom teacher and is derived from the author's years of experience both with teaching singing and in helping others to do so.

Sounds of Singing and *Sounds of Music*

Sounds of Singing has been carefully designed to be a free-standing course, for use on its own or in conjunction with a school's own music programme or other published resources. However, users of *Sounds of Music* – a classroom music scheme for primary schools – will see how easily the two resources dovetail together, resulting in a truly comprehensive solution for primary music education. More information about the relationship with *Sounds of Music* appears on page 91.

Universal links

Singing is universal. While there may be differences of expression in the curriculum requirements and guidelines of different countries, in essence they are much the same, and it is this common purpose that forms the basis of *Sounds of Singing*. Charts showing the correlation between the course and current curriculum documents are available free of charge. Please see page 91 for details.

The structure

There are three levels of *Sounds of Singing*: R–Y2/P1–3, Y3–4/P4–5, and Y5–6/P6–7. At each level there is a comprehensive teacher's book and a set of audio CDs.

The teacher's book is divided into chapters, concentrating on different aspects of singing, and each chapter is itself divided into lessons. An introductory page at the beginning of each chapter sets out the scope and focus of the lessons. The term 'lesson' is used loosely: you may indeed choose to teach all the suggested activities in one session, but equally you may prefer to tackle them in discrete chunks, perhaps in odd moments during the week or as part of a music lesson covering a broader range of topics.

Questions and answers

Within the lessons, questions have been devised for you to ask the children. The answers to these questions are in italicised brackets. The body of the text not only provides easily understood lesson notes but it also includes clarification and explanation of the more musically specialised matters.

Sequence, progression and differentiation

It is suggested that you teach the activities within a lesson in the order they are presented here, but it is not necessary to teach the lessons themselves in the printed sequence. All the lessons in *Sounds of Singing* are appropriate for the stated age range and there is careful progression from one book to the next. Within each lesson there is a wide range of activities that will suit all levels of ability, but much of the differentiation will naturally be by outcome.

Learning by rote

All activities for R–Y2/P1–3 are taught by rote. In Y3–4/P4–5 there are some references and learning experiences related to notation, and more again for Y5–6/P6–7. However, the most important and essential elementary skill is listening, because children cannot develop their singing without the ability to hear themselves, the group they are singing with, and their role models (teacher or recordings). You can, of course, use the given notation in any way you wish – however, the focus of this book is on aural skills.

Learning the words

Learning lyrics by rote is not a musical activity. This book aims to show you how to teach a song so that learning words for homework becomes obsolete. If you follow the lesson plans, the songs are taught in bite-size portions enabling the children to memorise one short section easily before going on to the next short section. The other learning method that is sometimes used, is to play the song as background music and let it slowly filter into the mind as if by osmosis.

Achievement

At the end of each lesson, 'achievement' points are identified to help you recognise what can be assessed and how effectively a child is developing his or her musical skills and understanding. Do not go into overload: at any one time, assess just a few children's achievements and focus on just one or two points.

What's on the page

The consistent, 'at a glance' layout of the lessons makes *Sounds of Singing* exceptionally easy to use.

ideas to help children warm up their voices and practise vocal techniques

clear objectives to focus teaching and planning

list of resources and background information to save preparation time

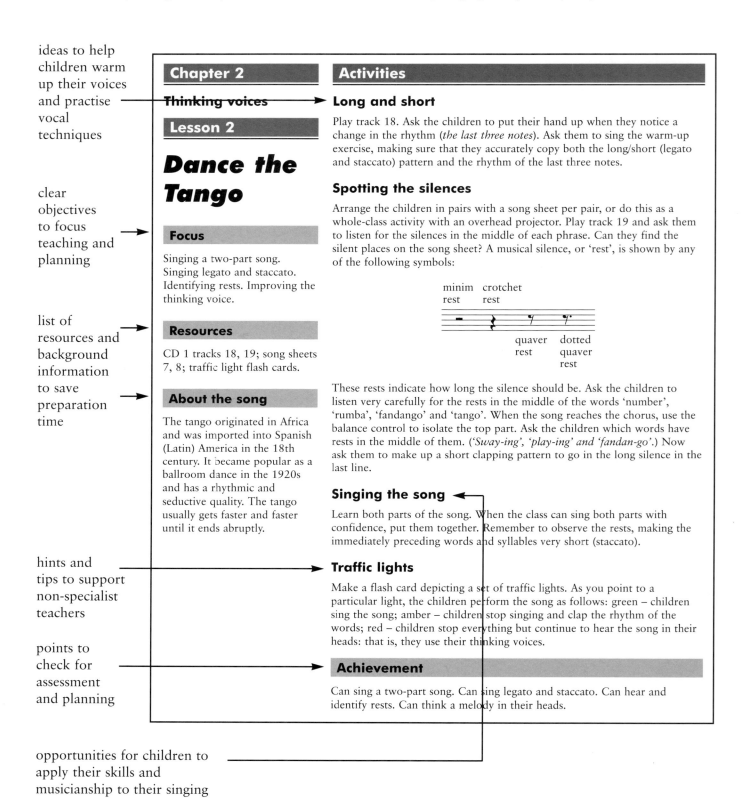

Chapter 2

Thinking voices

Lesson 2

Dance the Tango

Focus

Singing a two-part song. Singing legato and staccato. Identifying rests. Improving the thinking voice.

Resources

CD 1 tracks 18, 19; song sheets 7, 8; traffic light flash cards.

About the song

The tango originated in Africa and was imported into Spanish (Latin) America in the 18th century. It became popular as a ballroom dance in the 1920s and has a rhythmic and seductive quality. The tango usually gets faster and faster until it ends abruptly.

Activities

Long and short

Play track 18. Ask the children to put their hand up when they notice a change in the rhythm (*the last three notes*). Ask them to sing the warm-up exercise, making sure that they accurately copy both the long/short (legato and staccato) pattern and the rhythm of the last three notes.

Spotting the silences

Arrange the children in pairs with a song sheet per pair, or do this as a whole-class activity with an overhead projector. Play track 19 and ask them to listen for the silences in the middle of each phrase. Can they find the silent places on the song sheet? A musical silence, or 'rest', is shown by any of the following symbols:

minim crotchet
rest rest

quaver dotted
rest quaver
      rest

These rests indicate how long the silence should be. Ask the children to listen very carefully for the rests in the middle of the words 'number', 'rumba', 'fandango' and 'tango'. When the song reaches the chorus, use the balance control to isolate the top part. Ask the children which words have rests in the middle of them. (*'Sway-ing', 'play-ing'* and *'fandan-go'*.) Now ask them to make up a short clapping pattern to go in the long silence in the last line.

Singing the song

Learn both parts of the song. When the class can sing both parts with confidence, put them together. Remember to observe the rests, making the immediately preceding words and syllables very short (staccato).

Traffic lights

Make a flash card depicting a set of traffic lights. As you point to a particular light, the children perform the song as follows: green – children sing the song; amber – children stop singing and clap the rhythm of the words; red – children stop everything but continue to hear the song in their heads: that is, they use their thinking voices.

Achievement

Can sing a two-part song. Can sing legato and staccato. Can hear and identify rests. Can think a melody in their heads.

hints and tips to support non-specialist teachers

points to check for assessment and planning

opportunities for children to apply their skills and musicianship to their singing

In addition to the lesson plans, the book contains:

- song sheets which may be photocopied or projected for whole-class or group use
- advice on planning a singing session
- general advice on teaching singing
- a collection of generic warm-up activities which are not specific to any one particular song, but which can be used at any time
- general advice on the value of music, movement and dance
- a glossary of technical terms
- information about links with current curriculum guidelines and requirements, and with *Sounds of Music*
- an analysis of the songs and listening extracts.

The recordings

Recordings on audio CDs support each lesson. To get the best out of these recordings it is important to have a good CD player, preferably with a balance control. The quality of the sound makes a big difference to a child's response to any music. These recordings provide all the music mentioned in the lessons, including:

- **Warm-up exercises and games**
  These exercises prepare the voice for singing and teach specific vocal techniques. You might use these recordings to help you learn the warm-ups yourself, so that you can sing them with the children, or you might prefer to play the recordings directly to the class.

- **Listening extracts**
  Extracts of a wide variety of singing (and other music) for listening activities to focus children's attention on specific vocal issues. These extracts are of an appropriate length for the age group and for the activity and save you the time and money required to build and select from a large listening library.

- **Songs**
  Songs that are performed to a high professional standard and that provide an excellent vocal model.

- **Instrumental accompaniments**
  The instrumental accompaniments are varied, stylistically apt and musically satisfying. If your CD has a balance control you can isolate either the singing or the accompaniment, which are recorded on the separate stereo tracks. This enables the class to perform a familiar song with the professional backing track but without the support of the recorded vocals. Conversely, you may wish to focus on the vocal line when children are learning a song. Listening to the backing tracks on their own also gives a greater insight into the interpretation of the song, and many backing tracks can also be used as music for creative dance.

Please note that it is illegal to make copies of the CDs under any circumstances. Additional CDs are available.

All about planning a singing session

The following tips may help you to plan a well-structured singing session:

Space

Make sure that you have enough space for the children to stand comfortably.

To sit or to stand?

It is best to stand, but when the children do sit, please try to use chairs. It is really difficult to sing sitting cross-legged on the floor: it is like being asked to run a marathon with your legs inside a sack!

Ventilation

A room that is too hot, too stuffy or too cold will have a detrimental effect on any singing.

Know your material

Before you teach any song, you must know the piece intimately. It is said that amateurs practise until they get it right, but professionals practise until they can't get it wrong. You may not be a professional singer, but you are a professional teacher or choral leader and you need to know your song back to front so that you can teach it with confidence and detect exactly what the children are singing – both the good bits and the not-so-good bits. The lesson plans make this easy for you and will tell you how to approach the song as well as making you aware of any likely problems.

Admire your reflection

Using a long mirror to watch yourself singing and conducting is mentioned in 'All about singing', but it is worth reinforcing that it is one of the most helpful methods of becoming familiar with your material. Better still, ask a friend to take a video of you.

Make teaching simple

In truth, it is not possible to direct, listen, control and support a group satisfactorily at the same time as playing the piano. The piano acts as a sound barrier between you and the children, and your concentration is divided between the keyboard and the children. Teach a song from the recording, or use a guitar, or sing the melody unaccompanied for the children to copy.

Demonstrate, don't verbalise

Try to demonstrate rather than going into lengthy verbal explanations. Once the children have a reasonable grasp of the melody, stop singing with them and listen for any mistakes before they become too well established. Constantly remind the children to listen to themselves so that they blend in with everybody else.

Separate the tracks

If you have a balance control on your CD player, listen to both the backing track and the vocals on their own. The vocals provide a good role model and a standard of excellence for the children to copy. The accompaniments help to establish the mood, style and character of a song and help them with their expression and interpretation. Use the backing tracks to support the singing, not to drown it out.

General warm-ups

Before embarking on any strenuous physical exercise, it is essential to loosen up and to 'warm up' in order to prevent injuries. It is equally important to start each singing session with one or two general loosening and warm-up activities. Examples can be found on page xviii.

Specific warm-ups

The warm-ups that precede each individual song are devised in order to help address the more challenging aspects of that specific song. Many of these warm-ups can be transferred and used at the beginning of other singing sessions. For instance, articulation and pitch skills learnt in one song could be adapted and transferred to improve the execution of another song.

First things first

Ensure that the main teaching points are contained in the early part of the session while the singers are fresh. Use familiar material later on in the session to refocus and motivate.

Grouping

Sometimes it is advisable to select groups randomly: for example, by the colour of their hair, by birthdays, by the initial letter of their name, by their favourite food and so on. At other times you may want to distribute your stronger singers among the different groups.

Recording

Recording the class on tape or mini disk allows for evaluation and useful discussion afterwards.

Memorising

It is always best to perform any song from memory. This not only affects the sound quality (good posture is maintained) but it also means that you have constant eye contact with the children. When the children are looking forward, it establishes a rapport with the audience, engaging them with much greater effect.

Setting the scene

When practising, it helps to sing to an imaginary audience, perhaps to a romantic couple dining out, or to the family at home, or in a cathedral, or in the park. You will need to adapt your performance to each imagined (or real) situation.

High standards

Establish high standards – children like to be part of something that is successful.

Less is more

It is better for the children to sing one song really well than to sing four or five songs in a mediocre manner.

A satisfying end

End the session on a high. Make sure that the singers go away with a sense of achievement.

Extra-curricular choirs

Extra-curricular choirs need not run every week of the school year – this is a big commitment for both you and the children and they can become disenchanted with the routine. Form a choir for special events and rehearse for about six to eight weeks before the event.

All about singing

You can, of course, skip these introductory pages, and still succeed in teaching the contents of this book, but please do take some time to read them as it is here that you will find basic singing skills clearly defined, and written in plain English. The information will help you to understand how you can improve your singing and, as a consequence, it will increase your confidence – whether you are singing in the classroom, on a concert platform, in the crowd at a football match or simply in the bath.

The process of singing

The process of singing is quite straightforward to understand:

- Lungs supply the air.
- Air causes vocal cords to vibrate which creates sound.
- Sound is amplified by resonating cavities i.e. nose, mouth, neck and chest.
- The tongue, lips and teeth articulate the sound.

Posture

Stand in an alert and balanced position with a long spine and knees very slightly flexed – i.e. not rigidly locked. Your head should be level and aligned with the spinal column. Your chest should be raised and your shoulders down and relaxed with your hands by your side. Aim for balance and freedom, not rigid and soldier-like with chest puffed out.

When sitting on a chair, sit forward, feet flat on the ground, adopt a good posture to keep the chest and lungs upright in order to maximise the lung capacity. If you sit back in a chair, your body will take on the shape of the chair, which makes unrestricted breathing difficult.

A smiley face

Sing with a smiling face – not a great big grin but more as if you are breathing in the scent of a sweet smelling rose: you are surprised at the delicious aroma. This expression lifts the whole of your face and not only does it look good, but it also feels good and helps to keep the singing in tune and create a pleasant tone.

All about breathing

There are three parts to successful breathing whilst singing:

1. breathing in
2. breathing out
3. breath management.

Three sets of muscles manage the flow of air:

1. the diaphragm, i.e. the muscle that separates your lungs from your stomach and which supports the lungs like an elastic platform.
2. the intercostal (rib) muscles above the diaphragm.
3. the abdominal muscles below the diaphragm, i.e. between the diaphragm and pelvis.

Together these muscles manage the flow of air provided to the vocal cords (in the larynx). This air causes the vocal cords to vibrate and a sound is produced. In a child, the vocal cords are like two fine and delicate flexible threads; in adults they are more like two pieces of a rubber band.

Breathing in

When we go about our normal daily business, we breathe without thinking about it. We take in a small amount of air and only use the top part of our lungs. When singing, we need to sing long notes and phrases, so we must have a plentiful supply of air. To acquire this, we will need to breathe deeply and utilise our full lung capacity.

When we breathe deeply, the abdominal muscles expand, the intercostal muscles open up the chest (including the sides and the back) and air floods in saturating the whole of our lungs from the bottom to the top. Think of it as filling a bottle with water. The shoulders should stay relaxed and still. We do not breathe with our shoulders.

To actually see how your physiology changes, stand in front of a mirror. Put one hand on your abdomen, below your navel, and the other hand on your side around your waist. Breathe in deeply through your mouth and nose. Can you see your abdomen, sides and chest expand and your shoulders stay still? Another way to feel this is to lie on your back on the floor and to put a small book on your stomach. Breathe in deeply and watch the book move. Yet another way to locate your abdominal muscles is by bending right over in your chair and breathing deeply in and out. You will feel the muscles expanding and contracting.

Breathing out and breath management

We have already seen that when we breathe in without thinking about it, we take small amounts of air into the top of our lungs. So, when we breathe out without thinking about it, the lungs and ribs 'collapse' and the small amount of air, flows out.

We have also already established that when we sing, we need a lot of air in the lungs, however, we do need to ration the amount of air we expel, commensurate with exactly how much we need to use at any given time. To do this, we use our abdominal muscles to push air out of our lungs and to regulate the flow. Think of the lower abdominal muscles being the engine, and the air the petrol; the one controls the rate at which the other is used. Try putting your hand just ten centimetres in front of your mouth. Take a deep breath and blow on to your hand as if you were blowing up a balloon. Keep blowing a steady, even pressured stream of air until all the air has been used up. Keep your chest lifted and buoyant so that your ribs remain expanded, ready for the next intake of breath. Can you feel your abdominal muscles pushing the air out from the bottom of your lungs? Coughing quite vigorously may help you to locate those muscles and the associated physical sensation.

This controlled pressure from below the lungs is known as 'supporting the breath'. Good breath control is the secret to making a good sound.

You will notice that small children often sing with a very breathy tone, breathing in frequently and totally at random. This is because they do not know how to control the amount of air they expel at any one time. Try singing any song that you know with a breathy sound and hardly any melodic vocal sound. Now sing the same song without the breathy sound but with as much vocal sound as possible. In order to sing with very little superfluous breath escaping, you will have exercised some control over the rate of air flow. To do this you will have used the same mechanism described above. With regular practice, breath management can be improved until the sound becomes true and clear and long phrases can be sung.

Helping children to improve their breathing and breath control

Key Stage 1

Delving into the physiology of breathing would not be appropriate. You simply need to encourage the children to adopt a good singing position, to breathe low down (use the water bottle analogy), and to make sure that they have enough breath (and not too much) to last for the length of the phrase they are about to sing. Try not to say 'Take a big breath', as they are likely to pull in their abdomen, their shoulders will rise, they will create tension in their neck and throat, and they will probably only use the top half of their lungs. In this stance, they will have little control over the use of their air supply, and they will not make a very good sound. In other words they will take in breath, in exactly the opposite way to the low breathing technique described above. The best way is to ask them to take a drink of air or to take a deep breath or to breathe into their tummies.

Years 3 and 4

The children should begin to have more understanding of how to manage their breathing. Many children will know how to breathe deeply, and some children will be able to use their 'tummy' muscles to support the airflow for specific notes (e.g. high notes) or phrases (e.g. long phrases) or dynamics (e.g. passages that get louder).

Years 5 and 6

All children should clearly understand the principles of good breathing, and should be able to recognise the advantages of good breath management. Many children will be able to exercise good breath control, but do not expect them to automatically do this all the time. Professional singers spend years perfecting their breathing technique. Aim for silent, deep breathing and unanimity of breathing within a choir. Encourage the use of the abdominal muscles for specific notes and phrases (e.g. as above and in quiet passages, when singing large ascending melodic jumps, for accented notes and for downward scale passages).

Head and chest voice

We do not sing with our chest or our head! Every instrument has to have a resonating chamber to amplify the sound and the voice is no exception. The two main resonating areas are the chest and the head.

It is not possible to sing high notes using the chest voice; a sudden unattractive drop in volume occurs when higher notes are reached. Try asking a group of children to sing fairly loudly up a scale and notice the difference between the quality of the sound of the lower notes to that of the higher notes.

The light head voice is the voice that children will naturally use and the one that can be used across the whole range and for all styles of music. Children's natural chest voice does not have a lot of power and is quite quiet; this is why they force the sound when singing lower notes in order to achieve a greater volume. They use a kind of 'shouting' voice.

There is a place in some pop or rock songs, for using this stronger 'shouting' or 'belt' type of voice, but for classes and choirs, it is generally not advisable. It puts a strain on the vocal cords, is tiring to sustain, has a limited range and is not very musical. The children singing on the recordings of *Sounds of Singing* only once use their stronger chest voice and that is in Years 3 and 4, in the song, 'At the Hop' for the words 'Oh baby'. Volume will develop with age and experience rather than with forcing the vocal cords to belt out a song. To help projection, remember to pay close attention to posture and to breathing and ask the children to sing out – i.e. to sing to the other end of the room, not to shout to the other end of the room.

Singing in tune

Flat singing (singing under the note) often occurs when there is insufficient breath and insufficient support for the breath. It can also occur when singers are tired, when the room is hot and stuffy, when notes are pitched too high, on repeated notes, on descending phrases or simply when children have not had sufficient time to listen to the exact pitches they are being asked to sing. Remedy the problem by doing some physical exercises to re-energise the class. Pay attention to posture and breathing, ask the children to stand whilst singing, and to sing fairly quietly so that they can hear themselves. Play the 'flat' phrase several times on a pitched instrument or ask the children to listen to the recording so that they can hear and re-learn the correct pitches.

Sharp singing (singing higher than the note) is less common than flat singing and often occurs when children are anxious, when they are trying too hard, when they are singing high notes or when they are not listening carefully enough. To remedy the problem, do some relaxing exercises before having another go and play the 'sharp' phrase several times on a pitched instrument or listen to the recording so that the exact pitches can be heard and re-learned.

Articulation

To articulate with clarity, your face will need to be very flexible and your lips, tongue and teeth should work overtime, especially when singing in a large group. Try singing through a stiff 'letter box' mouth – notice how difficult it is to sing and to form the words. Silently mouth a sentence to an imaginary person at the other side of the room, and note the facial movement and physical sensation that precise and energetic enunciation requires. This is what is required when we sing.

Unified vowels

Tone is produced and carried on vowels, and vowel sounds are controlled by mouth shape. Sing the following vowels (on one long note) and notice how the position of your tongue, and your mouth shape (especially inside your mouth), changes with each vowel.

i as in need
e as in Ted
a as in part
o as in boat
u as in toot

Ideally every one should pronounce their vowels in the same way to produce the best tone quality and the best blend within a group of singers. Listen carefully for vowels that are obviously not unanimous and decide on the best pronunciation for your group of children and for the style of the song.

Expression

Good dynamics and expression 'make' a song. When deciding on the expressive qualities that you want to include, look at the words, feel the mood and find the main climax of the whole song. You can never sing too quietly, but you can sing too loudly.

Phrasing

Ensure that the children take the right amount of breath for each phrase (and not too much) so that it can be sung expressively and not peter out through lack of breath. Don't be afraid to shorten the length of a note at the end of a phrase to allow sufficient time to breathe before the next phrase begins.

Listening and vocal co-ordination

Singing is a physical activity and is really only an extension of speaking since it uses the same apparatus. Most children will hear pitches correctly but some children's vocal apparatus will not replicate that pitch. This is usually because, at some stage in that child's development, he or she has not had the opportunity to sing and to practise that basic skill. Just as some people are more skilled than others are at skipping or catching a ball, so it is that some can control their vocal apparatus better than others can. You can help children to improve their listening and singing co-ordination by asking them to copy your voice as you sing long continuous sounds at a pitch that is comfortably within their natural singing range. This could be quite a low pitch. Gradually extend the range and the number of notes. Do not exclude them from singing; they cannot improve if they do not practise and they will also feel very isolated.

Conducting

When you conduct a song, you direct the performers by using a variety of non-verbal gestures. Apart from using your hands and arms, other gestures will include eye contact, mouthing the words, nodding your head, using facial expressions and using your whole body to indicate mood.

Try to find time to work out what conducting gestures you will want to employ throughout the song by practising with the recording and in front of a mirror. Don't get hung up about what you suppose the 'correct' conducting gestures are. As long as the children know what you are asking them to do, then you must be doing it right!

What is it all about?

Singing is about doing, experiencing and feeling but above all, it is about enjoyment.

All about warm-ups

Physical preparation

Singing is not just about using our voice box; it involves the whole of our body. We must maintain a good posture and we will use our abdomen, diaphragm and rib muscles when breathing. We use our facial muscles, our lips, tongue and teeth and, above all, our ears, which tell our bodies what we have to do to produce a beautiful, expressive sound. Our eyes and body language tell others of the feelings we wish to convey. It makes sense to prepare for this physical activity by warming up all the component parts.

Improving skills

Warm-ups are also for practising basic singing skills, in just the same way as an athlete or an instrumental player will practise their basic skills to improve their overall playing.

So, take at least five minutes to do one warm-up or two at the start of any singing session. Begin with a few body and facial flexing and relaxing exercises. Follow those with some vocal warm-ups. Constantly revisit the warm-ups and invent some of your own.

Here are a few suggestions:

But first . . .

You will probably be quite a lot taller than the children, especially those in R–Y4/P1–5. In an effort to see you, the children will stretch their necks and look up, making it difficult for them to sing. You can either direct from a chair or stand much further away from the group so that their heads are in a good position.

loosen up the body, the vocal cords and the inhibitions . . .

- stretch each limb
- shake out each limb
- flick the wrists
- tightly clench the fist or face or buttocks for ten seconds, and then relax
- march on the spot lifting the knees up high
- flop over like a rag doll, then slowly unfold from the bottom up, keeping the head down until last
- stretch up as tall as possible
- curl up as small as possible
- roll and/or shrug the shoulders
- give the person next to you a shoulder massage.

from the neck upwards . . .

- tip the head gently from side to side
- make faces to a partner (angry, sad, happy, surprised, excited, etc.) and ask them to copy
- vulgarly chew pretend bubble gum
- massage the face
- squeeze the eyes tight shut for five seconds and then open them as wide as possible
- roll the eyes
- stretch the tongue down to the bottom of the chin and up to the tip of the nose
- curl the tongue up
- let the tip of the tongue go round every bit of the inside of the mouth
- have floppy lips and make 'horse' sounds
- make popping sounds with the lips.

from the nose downwards . . .

- make a full, slow yawn with an open mouth – let the sound come out with a sigh as the air is expelled
- breathe in slowly counting 4, hold the breath for 4, breathe out counting 4
- do as above but breathe out to a count of 6, then to 8, then 10, then 12
- do as above and breathe out to the letter F, or V or S; do not let the chest collapse when exhaling – keep it high
- take a deep breath; bend/flop over and let the body hang like a rag doll; expel air on an 'sss' sound until every little bit of it has gone; straighten the back to an upright position, raise the arms out to the side and level with the shoulders whilst taking in a deep breath; relax and breathe out as if blowing out a candle
- hum any note at a comfortable pitch and keep the sound going for several minutes by asking the children to breathe whenever they wish
- pretend to blow up a balloon
- give a great big belly laugh
- make the longest sound you can make
- make the shortest sound you can make
- make a series of short sounds.

by buzzing to find the best singing place . . .

- using both index fingers, lightly touch both sides of the nose and sing the syllable 'ing'; feel the buzz
- hum any note with loose lips and try to get the same sort of buzz.

by using your heart . . .

- make a sad sound with a sad face and gesture
- make an angry sound with an angry face and gesture
- make loving, sarcastic, surprised, happy, funny, disgusting, rude, furtive sounds and gestures.

by using your imagination . . .

- make a smacking sound
- make a popping sound
- make wet, explosive, sucking, clicking, blowing, etc., sounds.

by reaching the extremes . . .

- make the lowest sound you can make
- make the highest sound you can make
- slide the voice from top to bottom; bottom to top
- trace in the air the contour of an imaginary roller coaster, and ask the children to mirror its pathway with their voices
- vary the speed of the roller coaster; let it stop at the very top of the track, or let it crash to the bottom
- enjoy yourself; sing as if you are relaxing in a hot steamy bubble bath; no one can hear you in this resonant room because you are the only one in the house
- sing as if you are a world famous opera star
- sing as if you were the latest and most adored pop idol.

by clarifying the diction

- hum and go into one of the following vowel sounds:
  - hummm – ee (as in me)
  - hummm – e (as in bed)

- - hummm – ah (as in part)
  - hummm – oh (as in goat)
  - hummm – oo (as in toot)
- purr like a cat (roll 'r's)
- rapidly repeat individual words that are difficult to enunciate one after the other such as chocolate, lips, intimate, pop
- sing tongue twisters to the tune of the William Tell Overture, such as 'fight a frog, fight a frog, fight a frog, frog, frog', or 'crush a crisp', or 'tittle tattle'
- sing, phonetically, two consonants up and down five notes: for example, 'p and t and p and t and p' or 'k and l', etc.

There are many more exercises you can do, but these should loosen up the body, vocal cords and the children's inhibitions.

All about music, movement and dance

The importance of action in relation to thinking and learning is well recognised. We learn by 'doing'. On average we learn:

- 10 per cent of what we read
- 20 per cent of what we hear
- 30 per cent of what we see
- 50 per cent of what we see and hear
- 70 per cent of what we say
- 90 per cent of what we say and do – (Herman Ebbinhaus) because it is the doing that engages not just our mind, but our whole body in understanding and internalising feelings and concepts which are generated by musical experiences.

Some songs and music are written for dance purposes, but it is almost impossible for our bodies not to physically respond to any sort of music. It could be a toe tap to the beat, a lively dance or simply an inner stillness and intensity that allows no movement at all. Whatever the physical response to this emotional stimulus, it is almost always a pleasurable experience and one which invites repetition.

There are many ways in which movement and dance can enhance the musical development of a child.

Dance	Music	Musical elements
concentration	concentration	
movement memory	musical memory	
stillness	silence	dynamics
qualities of movement	qualities of sound	timbre
differences in energy; gross and small motor movement	differences in volume	dynamics
speed in travelling	variety in speed	tempo
movement patterning	rhythmic and melodic patterning	duration and structure
regularity of movement	pulse	duration
movement sequences	rhythmic and melodic sequences	duration and structure
repetition of movements	rhythmic and melodic repetition	duration and structure
combination of different moves and pathways	layers of sound	texture
structure of a dance	musical structure	structure
motor skills, control and co-ordination	playing instruments	
spatial awareness	awareness of phrase length	structure
focused listening to translate movement into a physical, visible form	listening skills	
interpretative skills	interpretative skills	all the elements
sensitivity and emotional response to dance	sensitivity and emotional response to music	all the elements
creativity and imagination	creativity and imagination	all the elements
timing and anticipation	timing and anticipation	rhythm
awareness of others	working with others	

When creating a dance or movement for a song, let the words as well as the music suggest the steps and actions.

Keep the movements simple.

Rehearse until the dancers can perform as a group, i.e. as a single unit and not as several individuals.

Singing voices

This chapter focuses on building confidence in singing and introduces basic activities for developing children's singing voices.

It looks at the singing posture and includes simple exercises to help with breath control. It explores the use of different voices and sounds and invites children to listen to, and to copy, a chant, replicating the voice inflections.

It provides exercises and makes suggestions for ways to improve articulation.

There are opportunities for singing in small groups and for singing solos through the use of call and response songs and there are suggestions for activities to foster a musical response.

Lesson	Focus
Oh, Watch the Stars	Bouncing abdominal muscles.
	Taking in enough breath to sing a whole phrase.
	Singing quietly and with expression.
Mission Control	Making 'oo' and 'ee' sounds.
	Breathing through an open mouth and throat.
	Small group and solo work.
Asi Desh	Singing a call and response song.
	Articulating clearly.
	Copying inflections.
	Chanting with good ensemble.
Three Pirates	Feeling cold air on the back of the throat.
	Laughing like Santa Claus.
	Solo singing.
	Inventing new words for the response.

CHAPTER 1

Singing voices

Lesson 1

Oh, Watch the Stars

Focus

Bouncing abdominal muscles. Taking in enough breath to sing a whole phrase. Singing quietly and with expression.

Resources

CD 1 tracks 1, 2, 3; song sheet 1.

About the song

This song is an American spiritual with a gospel feel to it.

Activities

The children should be shown how to stand when singing and should stand for each of the activities in this lesson. (See page xiii.)

Listening and understanding snake sounds

Before teaching this lesson, please refer to the section on 'Breathing' in 'All about singing' on page xiv. Listen to tracks 1 and 2. Ask the children what the difference is between the two sets of 'ss' sounds. (*The set on track 1 is very quiet but the set on track 2 is loud and energetic.*) Discuss with the children how the different sounds are made. (*In the first set, the singer took a very shallow breath and did not use her abdominal muscles to help to push the air out of her lungs. In the second set she has taken air into the bottom of her lungs – like filling up a bottle with water – and pulled in her abdominal muscles to push the air out.*)

Making snake sounds

Stand the children in a circle and ask them to make some pathetic, feeble snake sounds as heard on track 1. Now ask them to copy the strong short snake sounds. It is a good idea to have practised this before giving a demonstration! Without raising your shoulders, breathe into the bottom of your lungs. Now breathe out making short, loud 'ss' sounds. Feel your abdominal muscles bouncing in and out. Ask the children to copy your demonstration and to make their 'ss' sounds short and loud. Practise this several times. Now ask the children to breathe in slowly, without raising their shoulders, and to fill up their lungs just as if they were filling a bottle of water from the bottom up. They should then breathe out as fast as they can, making a continuous, loud, hissing snake sound. You can hear this on track 2. The 'ss' sound creates resistance to the flow of air and requires the tummy muscles to pull in and thus support the breath.

Breathing and humming a phrase

Play the song on track 3. Ask the children to hum the melody along with the recording and to follow the breath marks on the song sheet. They should take a small 'snatch' breath in the middle of each phrase and enough breath into the bottom of their lungs at the end of each phrase to last over the next 4 word phrase. Remind them to keep their shoulders relaxed when they take a deeper breath. When the melody is secure, add the words. Make sure that all the children sound that last 's' of the word 'stars' simultaneously and do not run that 's' sound into the 's' at the beginning of the word 'see'. Also ensure that they sound the 't' of 'bright' simultaneously.

Quiet singing with expression

At no time should this song be sung loudly. End the first musical phrase by getting slightly quieter, make the whole of the second phrase slightly louder, maintain the volume through the third phrase, and end the song quietly.

Achievement

Can bounce abdominal muscles to make 'ss' sound. Can breathe deeply with relaxed shoulders. Can sing with expression.

Oh, Watch the Stars

American Spiritual
Words adapted by Alison Ley

1. Oh, watch the stars, see how they shine,_____ Oh, watch the stars, see how they shine._____ The_____ stars shine bright_____ in the mid-dle of the night. Oh, watch the stars, see how they shine.

√ = snatch breath

✔ = deeper breath

2. Oh, watch the stars, see how they run,

   Oh, watch the stars, see how they run.

   The stars run down at the rising of the sun.

   Oh, watch the stars, see how they run.

Chapter 1

Singing voices

Lesson 2

Mission Control

Focus

Making 'oo' and 'ee' sounds. Breathing through an open mouth and throat. Small group and solo work.

Resources

CD 1 tracks 4, 5, 6; song sheets 2, 3.

About the song

Mission Control has a catchy melody and is a great favourite of children of all ages.

Activities

Oos and ees

Tell the children to say 'oo–ee' several times. To make the right mouth shape to say 'oo', ask them to put their lips around their finger and then take their finger out. Say 'ee' by keeping as big a space inside the mouth as possible, and relax the face into a slight smile, not a flashing, toothy grin. Listen to tracks 4 and 5. Ask the children to describe the difference in sound between the two versions of 'oo–ee'. The first is a warm, pleasant sound, whilst the second is harsh and screechy. Play track 4 again and ask the children to join in, singing the 'pleasant' way. Give them an opportunity to sing the 'screechy' way too. The secret to singing it the right way is to sing quietly, not to point the chin in the air, to keep an open shape inside the mouth for both the 'oo' and the 'ee' and to move only the lips when changing from 'oo' to 'ee' – not the jaw.

Finding the oos and ees

Listen to the song on track 6 and ask the children to find the words that make an 'oo' sound and those words that make an 'ee' sound. Play the song several times until all the 'oo' and 'ee' words are identified. Now ask the children to sing the refrain only, focusing on making a pleasant sound on the 'oo' and 'ee' words. The large leap in the melody at the end of lines 1, 3, 8, and 10 needs to be carefully pitched.

Small group performance

Ask for volunteers to sing the verses. Have three or four children sing each verse. Try to include every child in the class and praise them all for having a go. Some children may like to sing a solo.

Cold air breathing

Ask the children to breathe in noisily, through open mouths, so that they can feel the cold air on the back of their throats – as if they were yawning. Now do the same, but without making a noise. Sing the song again, singing each phrase of the song in one breath. At the end of each phrase, the children should take enough breath to sing the whole of the next one. Opening their throats will help them to do this.

Achievement

Can make pleasant 'oo' and 'ee' sounds. Can feel the cold air on the back of their throat. Can sing in a small group or a solo.

SONG SHEET 2

Mission Control

Words and music by Carmino Ravosa

SONG SHEET 3

Mission Control (continued)

Space is wide o - pen and wait-ing for me._____

Refrain

So, Mis - sion Con - trol,_____ do you read me?

I real - ly don't take_____ too much room.

Mis - sion Con - trol,_____ do you need me

On the next trip_____ to the moon?

X = 'oo' and 'ee' sounds

2. I want to study the planets.
    I want to study the stars.
    I want to go up to Venus, or Mars. *Refrain*

3. I'm working hard, and I'm certain
    An astronaut's what I will be.
    The sky is the limit for someone like me. *Refrain*

(spoken) Mission Control, do you read me?
          I'll be seeing you in about twenty years.
          Until then, over and out.

Singing voices

Lesson 3

Asi Desh

Focus

Singing a call and response song. Articulating clearly. Copying inflections. Chanting with good ensemble.

Resources

CD 1 tracks 7, 8, 9, 10; song sheet 4.

About the song

A popular patriotic *Bhangra* or harvest dance song from the Punjab (in northwest India). It emphasises to young people the importance of behaving well and being proud of their country. 'Asi Desh' means 'Our Country'. It is a 'call and response' song.

Activities

Lip gymnastics

Ask the children to loosen up their facial muscles by making as many funny faces as they can. Play track 7 and ask the class to copy the lip blowing and letter sounds making sure that there is a clear difference between the sound of the letters 'B' and 'P'. They will need really loose lips to do this exercise. Now ask them to silently mouth any short sentence to a partner at the other side of the room. They will have to exaggerate the use of their facial muscles, facial expression, their lips and tongue, for their partner to be able to decipher what they are actually saying.

Chanting a rhyme

Play track 8. Ask the children what they notice about the way the rhyme is pronounced. (*It is articulated very clearly and liltingly with every consonant being lightly pronounced.*) Ask them to listen very carefully to all the inflections in the voice and to try and copy exactly the way the rhyme is said. They will have to get their lips and tongues moving very flexibly. Make sure the 'll's of 'will', 'till', and 'they'll' are all clearly heard. Practise this until the class ensemble is good and they sound like one person saying the poem. For a bit of fun, gradually speed up the pace of the rhyme until in the end it actually goes too fast for the children to say it properly.

Chanting the refrain

Play track 9. Ask the children to copy exactly the way the words are spoken. Listen to the song (track 10), and ask them to notice how every word that is sung is clearly articulated. When they sing the refrain it should reflect the style of the call – i.e. be clearly enunciated and with a slight nasal tone quality.

Achievement

Can recognise a call and response song. Can articulate with increasing clarity. Can hear different inflections in the voice. Can chant with others.

Asi Desh

Punjabi children's song

Refrain

As - i desh — di cha - ra - di — la - li

Lesson 4

Three Pirates

Focus

Feeling cold air on the back of the throat. Laughing like Santa Claus. Solo singing. Inventing new words for the response.

Resources

CD 1 tracks 11, 12; song sheet 5.

About the song

A sea shanty was a sailor's work-song. Shanties originated in the days of sailing ships. The 'shanty man' sat apart and sang the tune. The sailors joined in the chorus whilst pulling the ropes or pushing the capstan and thus secured rhythmic unanimity.

Activities

Santa Claus laughs

Play track 11. Ask the children to yawn noisily like the singer, so that they can hear and feel the cold air going down their throat. Next ask them to breathe in deeply, as they did when yawning, but this time to add the energetic 'ha's and 'ho's as they expel the air. When they can do this successfully, ask them to do the same thing again but this time to breathe in silently. If they are 'laughing' correctly, they should feel their abdominal muscles pulling in with each Santa Claus laugh.

Singing the refrain

Play the song (track 12) and listen to how much energy the singers put into the 'yo-ho's. Ask the children to use their abdominal muscles to make the 'yo-ho's full of energy emphasising the letter 'h' at the beginning of each 'ho'. Remind them not to shout.

Singing or playing a solo

If you have a balance control, remove the recorded vocals. Some children may like to sing the verse as a solo or in a small group, while others join in the response.

Inventing new words

Ask the children to invent some nonsense words for the refrain. The use of alliteration would help the words to flow. For example, the last line could be: 'Be doo be degger, Be doo be degger, be doo, be doo, be doo'. Use the balance control to remove the vocals from the recording and ask the children to sing their invented responses instead.

Achievement

Can feel cold air going down their throat. Can use their abdominal muscles to expel air in short sharp bursts. Can sing a solo. Can sing the response with energy without shouting. Can improvise a response using own invented words.

SONG SHEET 5

Three Pirates

Old English Sea Shanty

1. Three pi-rates came to Lon-don Town, Yo-ho!—— Yo-ho!——

Three pi-rates came to Lon-don Town, Yo-ho!—— Yo-ho!——

Three pi-rates came to Lon-don Town, To see the King put on his crown,

Yo-ho, you lub-bers! Yo-ho, you lub-bers! Yo-ho! Yo-ho! Yo-ho!

2.   They came upon a wayside inn, Yo-ho! Yo-ho! (2 times)
They came upon a wayside inn,
And said, 'Good landlord let us in.'
Yo-ho, you lubbers! Yo-ho, you lubbers!
Yo-ho! Yo-ho! Yo-ho!

3.   'O landlord you have lots of gold,' Yo-ho! Yo-ho! (2 times)
'O landlord you have lots of gold,
Enough to fill the after hold.'
Yo-ho, you lubbers! Yo-ho, you lubbers!
Yo-ho! Yo-ho! Yo-ho!

ABOUT CHAPTER 2

Thinking voices

This chapter introduces two-part work, firstly with a dramatic chant in two parts and then with a simple two-part song.

It looks at the use of instruments, body sounds, movement or silence to substitute words and phrases in order to focus on inner hearing (the thinking voice).

Listening activities are chosen to highlight silences in music, and to identify the symbols used to indicate those silences (rests).

Opportunities are provided to practise the use of dynamics by very gradually getting louder and by varying the use of the voice, and there are also exercises for singing in both a smooth (legato) and detached (staccato) manner.

The pentatonic scale is featured and includes ideas for inventing and singing pentatonic phrases.

Lesson	Focus
The Battle of Badon Hill	Developing the thinking voice.
	Performing a two-part chant.
	Performing expressively.
	Substituting words and phrases with untuned percussion patterns, body sounds, movement or silence.
Dance the Tango	Singing a two-part song.
	Singing legato and staccato.
	Identifying rests.
	Improving the thinking voice.
The Bamboo Tone	Staggering breathing.
	Listening, singing and playing pentatonic melodies in three parts.

Thinking voices

The Battle of Badon Hill

Focus

Developing the thinking voice. Performing a two-part chant. Performing expressively. Substituting words and phrases with untuned percussion patterns, body sounds, movement or silence.

Resources

CD 1 tracks 13, 14, 15, 16, 17; song sheet 6; untuned percussion (optional).

About the chant

This battle piece is an attempt to recreate the feel of the 'real' Battle of Badon Hill fought by Arthur in the late 6th century. The names of the war leaders are genuine. Badon Hill was probably a hill near Bath.

Activities

The thinking voice

Use track 13 to play a game. The class will hear 'Saxons marching' once. They should just *think* the next 'Saxons marching', *chant* the third and listen for the recording to come in again with the fourth. If the recording interrupts the class's chant, or if there is a gap, then the children are not chanting and using their thinking voices exactly in time and on the beat.

Recording	Silence	Children	Recording
Saxons marching!	(Saxons marching!)	Saxons marching!	Saxons marching!

Play the game with other chants: Riding from Camelot, galloping north! (track 14); Follow the Horse banner! (track 15); Send out the skirmishers, rattle your shields! (track 16).

Learning the battle cries by heart

Play track 17, **The Battle of Badon Hill**. When the children have heard the chant through several times, use the balance control to isolate the two parts and teach the children each part separately and from memory. Divide the class into two groups – Saxons and Britons. The numbers on the song sheet indicate how many times each section is repeated. Try putting the parts together (without the recording). The Britons come in after the Saxons have said 'Saxons! Saxons!'

Thinking the battle cries

This time the whole class should chant each part separately but keep silent for one or two sections (e.g. 'Bedwyr! Kei! Bedwyr Kei!' × 3, or 'Up to the Ridgeway' × 4) and just think those sections in their heads. Suggest variations on this theme: the children could think every other phrase in their heads, or play a drum, or put an action to some phrases instead of chanting them. When the children can use their thinking voices well, ask each side to make up their own version of their part in the battle piece, substituting words with drums, body sounds, movement or silences. All these activities will help to develop the children's inner hearing (their thinking voice).

Putting it all together

A real challenge would be to put together both groups' interpretation of their side of the battle chant with the Britons once again coming in after the Saxons have said 'Saxons! Saxons!' Remember to get gradually louder and be sure to keep a steady beat without increasing the speed.

Achievement

Can think a rhythm or word pattern in their head. Can perform a two-part chant. Can perform expressively. Can substitute words and phrases with untuned percussion patterns, body sounds, movement or silence.

The Battle of Badon Hill

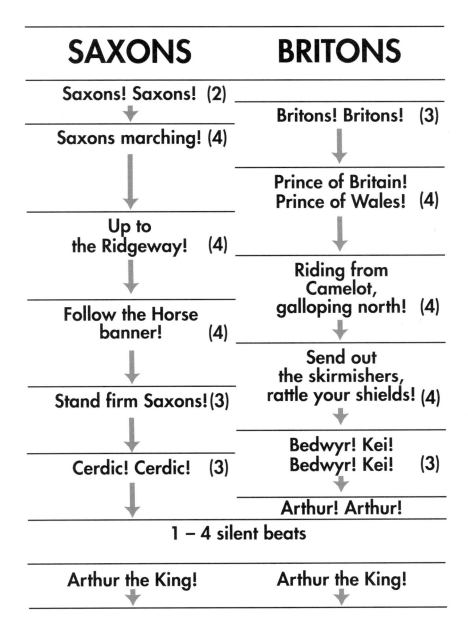

SAXONS	BRITONS
Saxons! Saxons! (2)	
↓	Britons! Britons! (3)
Saxons marching! (4)	↓
↓	Prince of Britain! Prince of Wales! (4)
Up to the Ridgeway! (4)	↓
↓	Riding from Camelot, galloping north! (4)
Follow the Horse banner! (4)	↓
↓	Send out the skirmishers, rattle your shields! (4)
Stand firm Saxons! (3)	↓
↓	Bedwyr! Kei! Bedwyr! Kei! (3)
Cerdic! Cerdic! (3)	↓
↓	Arthur! Arthur!

1 – 4 silent beats

Arthur the King! ↓	Arthur the King! ↓

Chapter 2

Thinking voices

Lesson 2

Dance the Tango

Focus

Singing a two-part song. Singing legato and staccato. Identifying rests. Improving the thinking voice.

Resources

CD 1 tracks 18, 19; song sheets 7, 8; traffic light flash cards.

About the song

The tango originated in Africa and was imported into Spanish (Latin) America in the 18th century. It became popular as a ballroom dance in the 1920s and has a rhythmic and seductive quality. The tango usually gets faster and faster until it ends abruptly.

Activities

Long and short

Play track 18. Ask the children to put their hand up when they notice a change in the rhythm (*the last three notes*). Ask them to sing the warm-up exercise, making sure that they accurately copy both the long/short (legato and staccato) pattern and the rhythm of the last three notes.

Spotting the silences

Arrange the children in pairs with a song sheet per pair, or do this as a whole-class activity with an overhead projector. Play track 19 and ask them to listen for the silences in the middle of each phrase. Can they find the silent places on the song sheet? A musical silence, or 'rest', is shown by any of the following symbols:

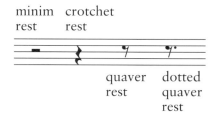

minim rest   crotchet rest   quaver rest   dotted quaver rest

These rests indicate how long the silence should be. Ask the children to listen very carefully for the rests in the middle of the words 'number', 'rumba', 'fandango' and 'tango'. When the song reaches the chorus, use the balance control to isolate the top part. Ask the children which words have rests in the middle of them. ('*Sway-ing*', '*play-ing*' and '*fandan-go*'.) Now ask them to make up a short clapping pattern to go in the long silence in the last line.

Singing the song

Learn both parts of the song. When the class can sing both parts with confidence, put them together. Remember to observe the rests, making the immediately preceding words and syllables very short (staccato).

Traffic lights

Make a flash card depicting a set of traffic lights. As you point to a particular light, the children perform the song as follows: green – children sing the song; amber – children stop singing and clap the rhythm of the words; red – children stop everything but continue to hear the song in their heads: that is, they use their thinking voices.

Achievement

Can sing a two-part song. Can sing legato and staccato. Can hear and identify rests. Can think a melody in their heads.

Dance the Tango

Joan K. Arnold

1. Ball - room dan - ces, there's a num - ber,

Pa - sa - do - blé and the rum - ba,

Ha - ba - ñe - ra and fan - dan - go,

But we're going to dance (× × × ×) the tan - go!

2.   Have you tried the waltz or quickstep?
    For the foxtrot there's a fixed step,
    In the Latin style you can go
    If you know the way to tango!

3.   Shimmy, twist and jives a-plenty.
    Charleston ruled in nineteen-twenty,
    Drums and cymbals they go bang-o,
    When we come to dance the tango!

SONG SHEET 8

Dance the Tango (continued)

Sounds of Singing Y3–4/P4–5 © Alison Ley, Nelson Thornes Ltd, 2003

Thinking voices

The Bamboo Tone

Focus

Staggering breathing. Listening, singing and playing pentatonic melodies in three parts.

Resources

CD 1 tracks 20, 21, 22; song sheet 9; tuned percussion.

About the song

This is a popular melody from China. It is about the New Year (Yuan Tan), celebrated in February with fireworks and gifts.

Activities

Identifying the Chinese style

Play track 20 and ask the children why **The Bamboo Tone** sounds so different from a Western popular song. (*Different instruments; the melody is played all the way through on a Chinese stringed instrument called an* erhu; *the bells and drum play the same rhythm all the way through.*) Explain that another reason why the song sounds different is because most Chinese music is based on a five-note (pentatonic) scale, whereas most Western music is based on an eight-note scale.

Drones and staggered breathing,

Play track 21 and teach the children to sing the drone. Divide the class, with one half humming the lower note (D) and the other half the higher note (A). To make a continuous humming sound the children will all need to breathe in different places, i.e. stagger their breathing. Before they run out of breath, they should decrescendo (get quieter) and then take in a breath. When they begin to hum again, they should do so quietly and slowly crescendo (get louder) until they are singing at the same volume as the rest of the class.

Pentatonic melodies

Now play track 22. The class will hear the drone again, then two short pentatonic melodies on their own, and finally the drone and the two melodies simultaneously. Draw the children's attention to how well the two individual melodies fit together over the drone; that is because all pentatonic pitches will fit comfortably with one another.

Composing and singing a pentatonic tune

Ask the children to work in small groups and make up a short (4- to 8-note) pentatonic melody on tuned percussion using any of the following the notes: $A_1 B_1 D E F^\# A B D^1$. Notes may be played more than once and in any order. The children should learn to sing their tune to 'noo'. Once each group has mastered this task, ask the rest of the class to hum a long continuous drone on the notes D and A (as above) and for each group in turn to sing their melody over the top of the drone. Experiment with creating silences (using their thinking voices) between each melody, and with combining some of the melodies.

Achievement

Can stagger breathing with control. Can sing over a drone. Can compose a short pentatonic melody.

SONG SHEET 9

The Bamboo Tone

Traditional melody from China
taken down from Zhao Ben
English words by George Odam

Here is the hap - py— time— of— wel - com - ing the New Year!

Child - ren and their fam - i - lies all ce - le - brate the com - ing of the spring.

Bang! Bang! the— fire— crack - ers sound, ech - o all— a - round.

Red are the pap - er flo - wers here in the win - dow, wel - com - ing the spring.

From the coun - try the play - ers— come. Laugh - ter and fun are all— a - round.

By the door our ban - ners— hang, wish - ing pros - per - i - ty and peace and joy.

ABOUT CHAPTER 3

Singing in time

This chapter has a more challenging two-part song, a Mexican song, which addresses the problems of singing foreign words and tackles the art of singing expressively.

It looks, in more detail, at singing and moving at the same time and recognises the importance of using movement as a way of feeling pulse and rhythm and of visually stating the structure of a song. By careful differentiation, it covers movement and left / right co-ordination for children at all levels of ability.

There are listening exercises to determine the metre of a song, and it includes a song which is partly in metre of 3 and partly in metre of 2.

There are opportunities for children to conduct the class and to set the speed (tempo) of a song.

Lesson	Focus
Music's Mine	Singing a song in two parts.
	Performing movements in time with the beat.
	Creating, rehearsing, performing and presenting a dance routine.
Dancing	Co-ordinating left and right whilst chanting.
	Singing a song and passing a bean bag in time with an accelerating pulse.
	Clapping word rhythms.
Piñata Song	Recognising a metre in 2, 3 and 4.
	Giving the words a Mexican feel.
	Singing with expression.
A Gest of Robyn Hode	Dancing a floral dance.
	Conducting and setting the tempo.
	Singing with robust energy.

Chapter 3

Singing in time

Lesson 1

Music's Mine

Focus

Singing a song in two parts. Performing movements in time with the beat. Creating, rehearsing, performing and presenting a dance routine.

Resources

CD 1 tracks 23, 24; song sheets 10, 11.

About the song

This is a recently composed song.

Activities

Loosening up

Ask the children to stand to do some physical warm-ups. Squeeze eyes tight shut and open them as wide as possible. Yawn and give a really big stretch. Roll the shoulders forwards and backwards, one at a time. Reach up high, flop over like a rag doll, and then stand up tall to a slow count of 6.

Learning the song

Play track 23 and talk about the words – particularly the meaning of harmony, melody, rhythm, texture and structure. Play the song through as background music during breaks or at other appropriate times during the day. Many children find that listening to background music whilst they work is helpful, pleasurable and calming, and over a period of time they will automatically absorb the words and the harmonies. If you wish to reinforce the individual parts, play track 24 and use the balance control to hear each part separately. When the children can sing both parts musically and from memory, divide the class in two and put both parts together.

Putting actions to words

Tell the children that they are going to make up movements to go with this song. Ask them to watch one of the 'pop' music programmes on television and to remember at least two of the moves that the 'pop' girl and boy bands perform to their songs. Ask for volunteers to demonstrate the moves they have remembered. Together with the whole class, select and order some of those moves to go with the song. Do not forget that some of the movements could be repeated, especially when the music is repeated. Try to select moves that are easy to remember, that flow easily from one to the other, and which exactly match the rhythm and tempo of the music. Some children will find dancing to the beat quite difficult. You may find it helpful to create a second dance sequence which is extremely simple, and which fits with the lower vocal part. The two routines could be danced together in the same way that the two vocal parts are sung together.

Performing and presenting

Work on this dance routine until it is well polished and runs smoothly. Ask the children to wear similar clothes e.g. (clean) jeans and a coloured tee shirt. Find a special time and occasion to present this to the rest of the school or to the parents.

Achievement

Can sing and hold a second part. Can invent appropriate actions to go with the music and words. Can perform actions to match rhythm and tempo. Can perform and present to an audience.

Music's Mine

George Odam

SONG SHEET 11

Music's Mine (continued)

 Sounds of Singing Y3–4/P4–5 © Alison Ley, Nelson Thornes Ltd, 2003

Dancing

Focus

Co-ordinating left and right whilst chanting. Singing a song and passing a bean bag in time with an accelerating pulse. Clapping word rhythms.

Resources

CD 1 tracks 25, 26, 27, 28, 29, 30; song sheet 12; one beanbag (or similar) per child.

About the song

A Slovak dance song.

Activities

Bongo knees

Sit the children in a circle. Ask them to pretend that their knees are bongo drums and that they are going to 'play' them with the recording. Play tracks 25–29, repeating each one several times until the children can correctly perform the left/right patterns on their knees. Ask them to chant the left/right patterns with the recording as they 'play' their knees. Some children may like to make up their own bongo knee pattern and lead the rest of the class.

Keeping in time with the accelerating pulse

Play the song (track 30) and ask the children what they notice about the tempo. (*Each repeat is faster than the one before.*) Invite the class to tap the pulse quietly, keeping in time with the increasing speed.

Chanting and clapping word rhythms

Teach the children the song words. If your CD player has a balance control you can use it to highlight the vocal part. Play the first verse repeatedly until the words and melody are known by heart. Ask half the class to tap the pulse on their knees while the other half claps the rhythm of the words. You might need to do this quite slowly.

Passing game

Sit everyone in a circle. Each player starts with a beanbag (or similar) in their right hand. Chant the song. On the first strong beat each player places their beanbag in front of the player to their right. On the next strong beat, they pick up the beanbag that has been put in front of them. (The strong beats are marked on the song sheet. Use only right hands, and move beanbags anticlockwise – another time you could use only left hands and pass beanbags clockwise.) Keep the beanbags moving, and practise this activity until the children can manage it well. Keep the tempo slow and steady. Eventually try playing the game with the recording. See how long the children can keep going steadily before the whole thing falls apart!

Achievement

Can co-ordinate left and right whilst chanting. Can sing, pass a beanbag and keep in time with an accelerating pulse. Can clap word rhythms.

SONG SHEET 12

Dancing

Slovak Dance Song
English words by George Odam

o = place beanbag in front of your neighbour.
x = pick up the beanbag in front of you.

Piñata Song

Focus

Recognising metre in 2, 3 and 4. Giving the words a Mexican feel. Singing with expression.

Resources

CD 1 tracks 31, 32, 33, 34, 35; song sheet 13.

About the song

Piñata Song is a traditional song from Mexico (probably originally from Spain). "Feliz Navidad, rompe la piñata!" means 'Happy Christmas, smash the piñata!' The piñata is a hanging bag which children smash to reveal gifts, fruits and sweets.

Activities

Recognising the metre of a song

Explain to the children that they will hear four songs and that they need to decide whether each is in metre of two, three or four. Ask them to pat their knees on the strong beat (first beat in every bar) and tap their hands on the weaker beats. Play track 31 (The Dargason, metre in 2, pat–tap); track 32 (Find the Ring, metre in 3, pat–tap–tap); track 33 (Rockin' Rockets, metre in 4, pat–tap–tap–tap); track 34 (Norwegian Mountain Dance, metre in 3, pat–tap–tap).

Piñata Song metre

Play the first section of **Piñata Song** (track 35) marked A on the song sheet. Ask the children to decide whether this section is in metre of 2 or in metre of 3 (*it is in metre of 3*). Ask them to pat and tap the metre, as above. Do the same with section B, which is in metre of 2. Divide the class in half and give each half one section to pat and tap, then swap.

Pronouncing the Mexican words

Play the song again and ask the class to listen carefully to the pronunciation of the Mexican (Spanish) words, especially the word 'piñata'. If your CD player has a balance control, use it to highlight the vocals. The children should practise rolling their 'r's to make sure that there is a good rolled 'r' on the word 'rompe'. The children will have to move their tongues and lips quickly in order to make the words clear and rhythmic. Throughout the song, make sure that they sing each phrase (line) in one breath.

Sectional colour

Ensure a good contrast between the two sections of the song. The first is more legato (smooth) and laid back; section B has a bouncing urgency about it which will be achieved by slightly emphasising the first beat in every other bar, and by accurately articulating the words. Encourage the children to have a slight smile (not a cheesy grin) as they sing – this improves the tone.

Achievement

Can recognise metre in 2, 3 and 4. Can roll their 'r's. Can sing with expression.

SONG SHEET 13

Piñata Song

Folk song from Mexico
Words by Nick Curtis

Christ - mas time brings chil - dren plea - sure,

Sounds of laugh - ter fill the air.

Take a swing at the pi - ña - ta,

Try and break it if you dare!

Fe - liz Nav - i - dad,____ Rom - pe la pi - ña - ta,

Fe - liz Nav - i - dad,____ Rom - pe la pi - ña - ta.

 Sounds of Singing Y3–4/P4–5 © Alison Ley, Nelson Thornes Ltd, 2003

Singing in time

Lesson 4

A Gest of Robyn Hode

Focus

Dancing a floral dance. Conducting and setting the tempo. Singing with robust energy.

Resources

CD 1 tracks 36, 37; song sheet 14; large space for movement.

About the song

The words come from a long 15th-century poem, 'A Lytell Gest of Robyn Hode'. Gest means a story or yarn and we still use the word 'jest' about telling funny stories. The melody is possibly as old as the poem and has been preserved in Cornwall where it is danced at the annual Helston Floral Dance to celebrate the coming of spring.

Activities

The Helston Floral Dance

The principal dance of the Floral Dance takes the form of a dignified procession, with the gentlemen wearing top hats and tails and the ladies in their finest dresses. Ask the children to find partners, to line up in a procession and imagine they are the dancers. As a class, make up a simple step dance to go with the song (track 36). Encourage the children to act the part and to dance with poise and dignity.

'Doo-be-doo'

Encourage the class to join in with track 37, singing the melody to 'doo-be-doo'. When the children can 'doo-be-doo' the melody by heart and unaccompanied, vary the tempo (speed) of the song. Do this by patting and clapping a pulse at a new tempo (pat–clap, pat–clap) and counting 1–2, 1–2 at the same time.

Conducting

Show the children how the tempo can be set by conducting the class. This song should be conducted in beats of two. To establish the tempo, count out two sets of two beats (1–2, 1–2) and conduct with small gestures for the first three preparatory beats (1–2, 1 – down up, down) but use a larger gesture for the fourth preparatory beat (up). Give a little bounce at the bottom of each downward beat to act as a springboard for the upward beat. Practise this beforehand with the recording and in front of a mirror. Ask for volunteers to stand in front of the class and try conducting. Try to give everyone a go, varying the speed from very slow to as fast as it can be sung or conducted.

Singing the words

Play track 36 and encourage the children to join in with the 'Holantoe' refrain. Teach the Old English words. If your CD has a balance control you can use it to highlight the vocals. This song should be sung in a lively and robust manner without shouting. A slightly stronger accent should be placed on the strong beats (Lythe, gen, be, blode, etc.), with the beginning of each word being very clearly articulated.

Achievement

Can dance in time to the music. Can set the tempo. Can conduct the class. Can sing robustly without shouting.

SONG SHEET 14

A Gest of Robyn Hode

Traditional melody
Words 14th Century English
Arranged by George Odam

28

ABOUT CHAPTER 4

Singing structures

This chapter looks more carefully at developing good breathing habits and at singing whole phrases without taking a breath in the middle. It provides exercises for singing long and short sounds, and a song to be able to practise the breathing for long and short notes.

There is work on vowels and consonants and on singing with a specific accent (in this case, Scottish).

There is an opportunity to sing a humorous song with the appropriate expression, and of moving to the 'off beat' in a lively Easter song.

The nasal hum is introduced followed by an African song which requires a 'forward sound'.

Through the use of movement and correct breathing, and by looking at the song sheets, it is possible to recognise and identify phrases, sequences, repetition and the overall structure of a song.

Lesson	Focus
Rainy Day	Recognising phrases, repetition and sequences.
	Expressing the meaning of a song.
Edward J Fox	Recognising and singing staccato, identifying phrases and singing them musically.
Three Craw	Singing with a Scottish accent.
	Rolling 'r's.
	Articulating clearly.
	Recognising repetition and sequences.
The Easter Bunny Hop	Playing on the 'off' beat.
	Recognising the different sections of a song.
	Accurately tapping and singing jumpy rhythms.
	Singing in a lively manner with good diction.
African Chant	Recognising different sections of a song.
	Placing the sound forward.
	Singing call and response.

Chapter 4

Singing structures

Lesson 1

Rainy Day

Focus

Recognising phrases, repetition and sequences. Expressing the meaning of a song.

Resources

CD 2 track 1; song sheet 15.

About the song

Rainy Day was specially composed for children.

Activities

Finding the phrases

Play track 1. Ask the children to listen for the phrases, and to draw 'rainbows' in the air to match the phrases they hear. Discuss the phrases marked on the song sheet. Are the phrases all the same length? (*Phrases 1, 2, 4 and 5 are the same length, phrases 3 and 6 are longer.*) Help the children to see that phrase 2 is a repetition of phrase 1. Phrases 4 and 5 are similar to 1 and 2 but start one tone higher – the musical term for this is 'sequence'. Some children may spot the differences between phrases 3 and 6 (different starting note, slightly different rhythm towards the end, phrase 3 goes up at the end, phrase 6 goes down).

Loosening up

Ask the class to stand and, keeping their shoulders down, to take in a drink of air that goes right down to their tummies. They should feel the cold air on the back of their throat. Now tell them to bend over, letting their bodies hang like floppy rag dolls, and to expel the air on a 'fff' sound. They remain in that position until desperate for air, when they slowly straighten their backs and stand up while taking in another deep breath. Repeat this exercise a few times.

Being expressive

Practise vocalising expressively by inviting the class to make sad sounds to match appropriately sad faces. Do the same for angry, surprised, happy, shocked, disgusted, secretive, etc.

Singing expressively

Play track 1 and discuss the meaning of the song. Are the recorded singers performing it with appropriate expression? Use the recording to teach the song and encourage the children to sing expressively. Try singing the song with sad/happy/angry/shocked voices. Which works best? Remind the children to breathe at the places marked and to make sure that they have just the right amount of breath for each phrase. Draw attention to the melody moving downwards in steps at the end and encourage them to sing in tune by asking them to take little 'snatch' breaths after the word 'sure' in both the first and second bars and by listening carefully to the recording as they sing.

Achievement

Can recognise a phrase. Can recognise repetition. Can recognise a sequence. Can discuss expressive singing and reflect the meaning of a song.

Rainy Day

George Odam

phrase 1

Look - ing out on the rain,

phrase 2

rain - y day yet a - gain!

phrase 3

Ev' - ry day when I want to play— out - side the clouds are grey.

phrase 4

Look - ing out on the rain,

phrase 5

rain - y day yet a - gain.

phrase 6

I'm as sure as I can be sure the sun will shine a - gain.

Chapter 4

Singing structures

Lesson 2

Edward J Fox

Focus

Recognising and singing staccato, identifying phrases and singing them musically.

Resources

CD 2 track 2; song sheet 16.

About the songs

Edward J Fox is a silly song written especially to appeal to children's sense of humour.

Activities

Long and short sounds

Invite the children to make the longest vocal sounds they can, and then the shortest sounds. They should listen to each other and discuss who can make the longest/shortest sounds. Play track 2 and discuss the humorous words and special effects (*cough, plane*). Play it again and ask the children to put up their hands when they hear especially long sounds (*air and way*). Do the same for especially short sounds (*fox, box, off, cough*). They could mark on the song sheet where they hear especially long and short sounds. Explain that a dot over or under a note indicates that it must be made shorter and more detached than usual (staccato).

Singing long and short sounds

Invite individuals, pairs or groups to sing **Edward J Fox** as humorously as possible, paying particular attention to the especially long and short notes.

Finding the phrases

Play the song again and ask the children to trace 'rainbows' in the air to show the phrases. Ask if the phrases are all the same length? (*Phrases 3 and 6 are longer.*) See if the children can spot the two identical phrases (*1 and 2*) and the two phrases which are very similar to them (*4 and 5*).

Putting it all together

Sing the song as a class, paying particular attention to the long and short notes. The children will have to listen carefully to their neighbours' singing in order to keep together. Encourage them not to take a breath in the middles of phrases 3 and 6. They will need to take in sufficient air at the beginning and control their air flow in order to have enough puff left for the long notes at the ends of those phrases. You could tape record their performances for them to appraise and improve upon.

Achievement

Can recognise staccato notes. Can sing especially short and long notes. Can recognise a phrase. Can control breathing to sing a phrase musically.

Edward J Fox

Words and music by Peter Combe

Ed - ward J. Fox Stands on a box, On the run - way in the mid - dle of the air - port. When the jum - bos take off He gives a lit - tle cough, Then he takes his box out of the way!

Chapter 4

Singing structures

Lesson 3

Three Craw

Focus

Singing with a Scottish accent. Rolling 'r's. Articulating clearly. Recognising repetition and sequences.

Resources

CD 2 tracks 3, 4, 5; song sheet 17.

About the song

Three Craw is a folk song from Scotland. The words may need some explanation.

Activities

Warming up the Scottish vowel sounds

Singing in a different accent requires the children to listen carefully to the different vowel sounds and to practise them so that they all end up singing the same sound. Listen to the singer warming up on track 3, and then ask the children to do the warm-up themselves. Mmm-ee (as in three), mmm-aw (as in craw), mmm-a (as in sat), mmm-or (as in cold). Encourage them to listen carefully to their own voices and to try and match the vowel sounds on the recording.

Rolling 'r'

The Scottish accent has a very strong rolled 'r'. Use the balance control with track 5 to play only the vocals and ask the children to identify at least two words which have a rolled 'r'. (*three, craw, frosty and morning*). Look at the warm-up exercise from Chapter 7 lesson 3. Play track 4 and ask the children to copy the singer. Now practice the 'r's found in **Three Craw** – i.e. thrr, crr, frr, and morr.

Singing the song

Use track 5 to teach the song. Encourage the class to join in with the children on the recording, and eventually to sing the whole song. Ask the children to articulate the words as crisply as they can, copying the clear diction of the singers on the recording and trying to roll their 'r's. Individuals, pairs or groups could take it in turn to sing the verses.

Listening to the structure

Ask the children if they can hear any sequences in the song, i.e. the same melody pattern but at a different pitch. (*The four repetitions of 'sat upon a wa'', 'could na' find his maw', etc. are sequences.*) They could use the song sheet to check their answers.

Achievement

Can sing vowels with the appropriate accent. Can sing rolled 'r's. Can articulate clearly. Can recognise a sequence.

Three Craw

Folk song from Scotland

1. Three craw sat up-on a wa',
Sat up-on a wa', Sat up-on a wa',—
Three craw sat up-on a wa',
On a cold and frost-y morn-ing.

2. The first craw could na' find his maw,
Could na' find his maw,
Could na' find his maw,
The first craw could na' find his maw,
On a cold and frosty morning.

3. The second craw could na' find his paw,
Could na' find his paw,
Could na' find his paw,
The second craw could na' find his paw,
On a cold and frosty morning.

4. The third craw ate the other twa,
Ate the other twa,
Ate the other twa,
The third craw ate the other twa,
On a cold and frosty morning.

5. The fourth craw warna' there at aw,
Warna' there at aw,
Warna' there at aw,
The fourth craw warna' there at aw,
On a cold and frosty morning.

6. That's aw I hear about the craw,
Hear about the craw,
Hear about the craw,
That's aw I hear about the craw,
On a cold and frosty morning.

Chapter 4

Singing structures

Lesson 4

The Easter Bunny Hop

Focus

Playing on the 'off' beat. Recognising the different sections of a song. Accurately tapping and singing jumpy rhythms. Singing in a lively manner with good diction.

Resources

CD 2 tracks 6–18; song sheets 18, 19.

About the song

This children's song is about the traditional 'hunt the Easter egg' game, where the eggs are supposed to have been hidden by the Easter Bunny. Although Easter is a Christian festival, both eggs and bunny (originally a hare) come from Celtic (non-Christian) spring festival traditions.

Activities

Feeling the 'off' beat

Listen to track 6, **The Easter Bunny Hop.** To enjoy the jazzy feel of this song, do this activity with the class. Sitting down, hold your left hand about 20cm above your lap, palm down. Slap your thigh with your right hand, and then move the right hand upwards so it pats the palm of your left hand. Keep doing this (thigh, hand, thigh, hand) to a steady beat of 4. Now play track 6 and ask the class to do the slap–pat action to the steady beat. Start after the introduction with a thigh slap on 'Where'. When the children have practised this, suggest they keep doing the same movement but don't actually touch their thighs. This will leave only the pat on the 'off' beat (1 – pat, 3 – pat). Practise with the recording until the children are confident.

Listening for the structure

Show the class the lyrics on song sheets 18 and 19. Discuss what they mean and then ask the children what they notice about the structure. (*The beginning and end sections are the same.*) Play track 6 and ask the children to listen carefully to the melody. What do they notice about the beginning and end sections? (*They are the same.*) Introduce or revise the term 'ABA' to describe this structure, depending on the children's prior knowledge. A is the beginning section, B is the different, middle section, then A is repeated.

Practising rhythms

The character of this song depends on singing the rhythms accurately, or the bunny doesn't hop! Use tracks 7–12, which demonstrate some of the word patterns used in the song. Each pattern is spoken twice. Pause after each pattern for the children to chant precisely what they hear. Practise until the class can chant completely in unison, and not sound like many individuals. Now play tracks 13–18, which contain the same rhythms tapped, without the words. Pause after each track for the children to identify the pattern, and ask them to copy by tapping two fingers in the palm of the hand. Clapping is too heavy a sound and too large a movement to be able to reproduce the rhythms accurately. Again, practise until the rhythms are as good as they can be.

Singing the song

Invite the class to sing with track 6. Try to copy the recorded vocals – lively and tight, with clearly articulated words and, above all, rhythm.

Achievement

Can pat on the 'off' beat. Can accurately tap and sing dotted (jumpy) rhythms. Can sing with expression and clear articulation.

The Easter Bunny Hop

George Odam

Where did he hide— them?— What is in-side— them?— Those

bright - ly col - oured paint - ed— chick - en's eggs.

Here comes— the East - er Bun - ny,— hop - ping—

hop - ping in and out of the flowers—

Croc - us - es yel - low;— what a fun - ny fel - low,—

trip - ping in and out the daf - fo - dils. The

SONG SHEET 19

The Easter Bunny Hop (continued)

Singing structures

African Chant

Focus

Recognising different sections of a song. Placing the sound forward. Singing call and response.

Resources

CD 2 tracks 19–23; song sheet 20.

About the song

African Chant is a call and response song. The nonsense words are a mixture of a West African language and French.

Activities

Moving to the structure

African Chant is a song in three sections (numbered 1, 2 and 3 on the song sheet). Each section consists of a call and response, and is sung twice. Play track 19 all the way through and ask the children to listen for the call and response and the three different sections – provide the song sheet for them to follow the notation. Organise the class into three groups and number them 1, 2 and 3. Ask the children to stand (or make some other agreed movement) when their section is sung and to keep still during the others. Play this game a few times, swapping the numbers and varying the actions.

The singing nose

Listen to track 20. The singer is using the sound 'ing' (with the silent 'g') to make a nasal hum. She is singing forward and not in the back of her throat. Ask the class to imagine the singing place being where they would blow their nose, and to copy the nasal hum. Play track 21. Here the singer keeps the nasal hum on the sound 'ing', and gently moves around her vocal range. Ask the class to keep thinking about the singing nose and, using the 'ing' sound, to follow your hand movements as you gracefully move them up and down. Finally, play track 22 and ask the children to copy the 'ning-nang' exercise, still keeping a forward nasal sound, and letting each word ring.

Learning and singing call and response

Play track 19 and ask the children to listen very carefully to the forward nasal sound the singers make, especially the solo singer in the call section. Practise singing the refrain unaccompanied and very slowly to the word 'ning'. Ask the children to keep the same forward nasal sound that they practised in the warm-up exercises. Once you are happy with the accuracy of the pitch, play track 19. Either use the balance control (if you have one) to play just the call, or play only the backing track so that you can sing the call yourself, and ask the children to sing the response with the proper words. Teach the call in the same way, but make sure the children sing with a forward tone and do not force their voices when trying to sing loudly.

Performance

When the vocals are secure, divide the class into two groups (call and response) and invite them to sing the song either unaccompanied with a steady drum beat as an accompaniment, or accompanied only by the backing track (track 23). Add some suitable relaxed movement.

Achievement

Can recognise the structure of the song. Can sing with a nasal quality. Can sing call and response.

SONG SHEET 20

African Chant

Traditional

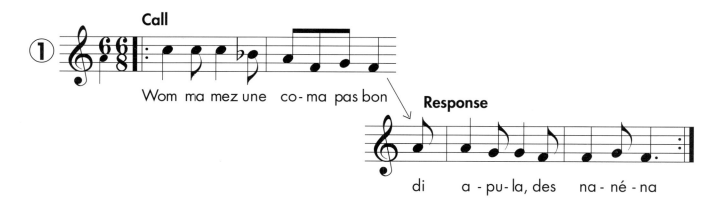

Call
Wom ma mez une co-ma pas bon

Response
di a - pu-la, des na - né - na

Call
nez à ba di a - pu - la

Response
di a - pu-la, des na - né - na

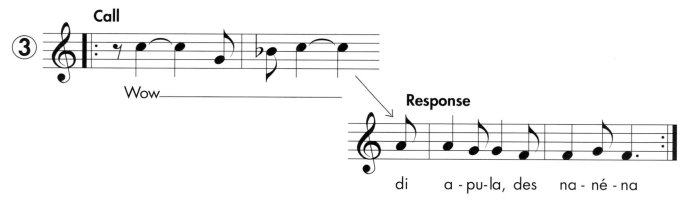

Call
Wow

Response
di a - pu-la, des na - né - na

Sounds of Singing Y3–4/P4–5 © Alison Ley, Nelson Thornes Ltd, 2003

Singing the notes

This chapter focuses on the effect of singing a song using different starting notes, on listening, recognising and accurately pitching leaps within a song, on using hand movements to show when notes go higher or lower, and on decoding music notation and recognising the contour of a melody.

There are some tongue gymnastics, tongue twisters and subsequent work on articulation.

Great attention is given to ways of injecting vibrant and meaningful expression into a song, and of singing in a particular style – in this case with a 'swing' and an American accent.

An easy round is introduced with helpful pointers on how to teach a round and the different ways of dividing up the 'parts'.

Lesson	Focus
Oliver Cromwell	Loosening up the tongue.
	Chanting and singing a tongue twister.
	Pitching the notes accurately.
	Changing the pitch of a song.
Baba Yaga	Listening for, and then discussing, musical features and feelings.
	Telling a story with expression.
	Singing with expression.
	Using hand movements to reflect melodic leaps and stepwise movement.
Everybody Loves Saturday Night (1)	Recognising and identifying direction in melody, repetition and sequences.
	Decoding and using staff notation.
	Singing in parts.
I'm Gonna Sing	Decoding staff notation.
	Singing with an American accent and with a 'swing'.
	Adding movement to the performance.

Chapter 5

Singing the notes

Lesson 1

Oliver Cromwell

Focus

Loosening up the tongue. Chanting and singing a tongue twister. Pitching the notes accurately. Changing the pitch of a song.

Resources

CD 2 tracks 24, 25, 26, 27; song sheets 21, 22.

About the song

Oliver Cromwell is a traditional Suffolk folk song.

Activities

Tongue gymnastics

Invite the children to do this warm-up activity, introducing these instructions as you think fit! Stick your tongue in and out very quickly, several times. Now try to touch your chin/nose/ears with your tongue. Take the tip of your tongue for a walk all around the inside of your mouth. Curl up your tongue and then quickly unfurl it and point it at the ceiling.

Peter Piper

Play track 24 and help the children to learn **Peter Piper** from memory. Chant it very slowly at first and keep the speed steady. Do not be tempted to chant any faster than the children can comfortably manage. Make sure that all the words are crystal clear with everybody working their lips and their tongues overtime. Every consonant should be heard – including the letter 'l' in pickled. Play tracks 25 and 26. Ask the class what differences they notice each time the chant is sung. (*Changes in speed and pitch*.) Does Peter Piper's tune move smoothly by step, or in leaps? (*Leaps*.)

Singing big leaps in tune

Help the children to learn Peter Piper's first tune by heart, listening very carefully to track 25. (*You could also sing it or play it on a tuned instrument*.) The children should sing slowly and quietly so that they can hear themselves and concentrate on pitching the right note. (Not every child will be able to sing in tune – but this type of practice will focus their minds on hearing the right pitches and over time they will improve.) Sing the rest of Peter Piper's tunes (track 26). Discuss the effect of making the starting notes higher and lower. Are all Peter's tunes as easy (or difficult) to sing as each other? If not, why not?

Oliver's jumps

Play **Oliver Cromwell** (track 27). Ask the children to listen for the similarities between Peter's tune and Oliver's tune. (*Both have lots of words to be fitted into a short space and both melodies use mostly the same notes*.) This song is best sung quite fast, so practise it unaccompanied and more slowly at first until the words are clear and the melody is secure and accurately pitched, then sing it with the recording. Choose different starting notes when singing unaccompanied, and ask the children what effect this has on the song. Hum the starting note first so they all concentrate on matching the pitch before they begin to sing the song.

Achievement

Can chant a tongue twister pronouncing all the consonants with clarity. Can pitch notes with accuracy. Can start a song on different notes.

Peter Piper

Words traditional
Music Alison Ley

Pe - ter Pi - per picked a peck of pick - led pep - per A

peck of pick - led pep - per Pe - ter Pi - per picked If

Pe - ter Pi - per picked a peck of pick - led pep - per

Where's the peck of pick - led pep - per Pe - ter Pi - per picked?

SONG SHEET 22

Oliver Cromwell

Traditional Suffolk folk song

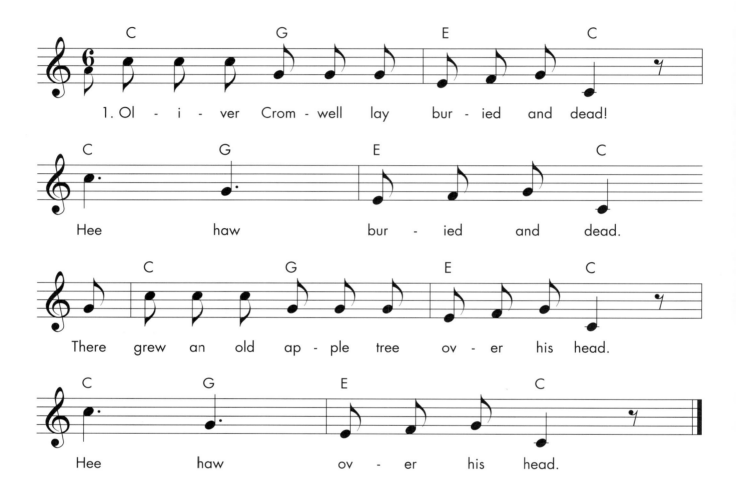

2. The apples were ripe and ready to fall.
   Hee haw ready to fall.
   There came an old woman to gather them all.
   Hee haw gather them all.

3. Oliver rose and gave her a drop.
   Hee haw gave her a drop.
   Which made the old woman go hippetty hop.
   Hee haw hippetty hop.

4. The saddle and bridle they lay on the shelf.
   Hee haw lay on the shelf.
   If you want any more you can sing it yourself!
   Hee haw sing it yourself!

Sounds of Singing Y3–4/P4–5 © Alison Ley, Nelson Thornes Ltd, 2003

Lesson 2

Baba Yaga

Focus

Listening for, and then discussing, musical features and feelings. Telling a story with expression. Singing with expression. Using hand movements to reflect melodic leaps and stepwise movement.

Resources

CD 2 tracks 28, 29; song sheet 23.

About the song

Baba Yaga is based on a Russian folk tale about a little girl called Natasha. The wicked Baba Yaga, who grinds up her victims in a pestle and mortar and eats them, captures Natasha, but she manages to escape.

Listening to the song

Introduce the Baba Yaga story (see 'About the song') and listen to track 28 several times. Focus attention by asking questions about the words. Then ask the class to listen to the instrumental backing and describe what they hear. (*The notes move fast, they are slightly detached, there is a lot of clashing percussion, the timbre (colour) of the tune sounds thin and mean.*) If your CD has a balance control you can remove the vocal track to highlight the accompaniment.

Listening to the vocals

Ask the children to listen carefully to the recorded vocals (using the balance control if you have one) and then discuss the way the melody is sung and the way the words are expressed. (*It is sung in a slightly detached (staccato) manner. The words are sung with enormous energy; the initial 'B' and 'Y' of Baba Yaga are given extra emphasis, as is the 'sh' in Natasha. All the words are 'spat out' – the feeling is of someone in a hurry and in a real panic.*)

Telling the story

Listen to track 29 and notice how much passion and urgency the reader puts into the story. The children should work in pairs: one child should read the story to the other (song sheet 23), and then swap. They should use a great deal of vocal, facial and bodily expression, as if they are warning Natasha to flee away from Baba Yaga. Some children may find it easier to tell the story in their own words. Then ask the children to sing the song with track 28, using as much energy and expression as they can muster and making the words very clear.

Steps, leaps and moving hands

The melody in **Baba Yaga** moves mostly by step – reflecting Natasha running away? Show the children the stepwise notes marked on the song sheet. Also show them the big leap at the beginning of the song – perhaps Natasha leapt up in the air before she started running. Play track 28 and ask the class to move their hands in the air, from low to high, to match the jumping notes at the beginning of the song, and to follow the stepwise movement of the running notes.

Achievement

Can describe what they hear. Can tell a story with real passion. Can sing with expression. Can use movement to reflect the melodic line.

SONG SHEET 23

Baba Yaga

George Odam

KEY

⌐‾‾‾⌐ = stepwise movement

Singing the notes

Everybody Loves Saturday Night (1)

Focus

Recognising and identifying direction in melody, repetition and sequences. Decoding and using staff notation. Singing in parts.

Resources

CD 2 tracks 30, 31; song sheet 24.

About the song

This traditional song from Ghana may be sung as a round.

Activities

Rollercoaster warm-up

Trace the contour of an imaginary rollercoaster with your hands in the air, and ask the class to follow the ups and downs with their voices. (Ensure the children are 'reading' from left to right.) Constantly vary the speed; make the rollercoaster stop at the very top of the track; let it crash to the bottom. Let children take turns at being the conductor.

Identifying direction in the melody

Listen to track 30 a few times, and invite the children to trace the direction of the melody in the air with their hands, or on the whiteboard, or with a pencil on paper. Compare the children's tracing with the arrows on the song sheet. Help the children to see that the placing of the notes on the staff reflects the direction of the arrows – the higher the note is placed on the staff, the higher it sounds.

Decoding the notation

Encourage the class to answer these questions by referring to the notation on the song sheet, and then check up by listening to track 30. Can you find places in the notation where notes are repeated? (*The four notes on the word 'ev-'ry-bo-dy'.*) The word 'everybody' is sung seven times. How many times is it sung at the same pitch? (*The first and last times.*) What happens to the melody in line 3? (*It moves downwards by step.*) Are there any sequences? (*Line 2 is a sequence of line 1; line 3 contains four sequences.*)

Singing the round

Listen to track 31 and ask the children what they notice about it. The song is sung through once and then, after a short instrumental interlude, it is sung as a round. The singers are divided into four groups, each singing the song but with a staggered start, so group 2 begins line 1 when the first group reaches line 2, and so on. You can achieve the same effect by dividing the class into four and allocating one line to each group; each group simply repeats their line throughout the duration of the 'round'. A conductor controls the performance, indicating when each group should start and stop and varying the dynamics (indicating when to sing quietly/loudly). Put together a class performance, involving the children in planning how many times the song will be sung through and how the dynamics should vary.

Achievement

Can identify direction in melody, repetition and sequences both aurally and from staff notation. Can hold a vocal part. Can contribute to a class performance.

SONG SHEET 24

Everybody Loves Saturday Night

Folk song from Ghana

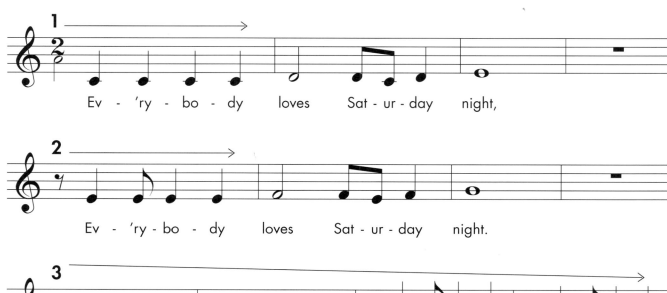

Ev - 'ry - bo - dy loves Sat - ur - day night,

Ev - 'ry - bo - dy loves Sat - ur - day night.

Ev - 'ry-bo - dy, Ev - 'ry-bo - dy, Ev - 'ry-bo - dy, Ev - 'ry-bo - dy,

Ev - 'ry - bo - dy loves Sat - ur - day night.

48

Chapter 5

Singing the notes

Lesson 4

I'm Gonna Sing

Focus

Decoding staff notation. Singing with an American accent and with a 'swing'. Adding movement to the performance.

Resources

CD 2 tracks 32, 33; song sheets 25, 26.

About the song

This is a traditional gospel song.

Activities

Deciphering the code

Make sure all the children can see the notation on song sheet 25. Read aloud the passage on sheet 26, or play CD 2 track 32, to help the class to identify these elements of the notation: time signature; staff; notes of different duration; rests.

Following the notation

Listen to the song on track 33. Ask the children to look at the notation and they will see that the music for the beginning of the first three lines (phrases) is exactly the same. Ask them to identify where the melody is different in the first three lines. (*The notes for the word 'sing' right at the end of each phrase.*)

Getting that gospel feel

Invite the class to join in with the children on track 33. The vocals are sung with an American accent, especially noticeable on the words 'spirit of the' and 'dance'. Ask the children to copy that accent, and also to hang on to the very last note for as long as the recorded children. The movement suggestions below will help the children to catch the spirit of the song and sing it with a swing.

Moving and grooving

Gospel songs and spirituals are enhanced with movement. Help the class or groups to create some simple step and hand movement to go with the feel and steady beat of the song. (For example, 1: transfer weight from one foot to the other; 2: bend knees alternately; 3: click fingers or clap on the 'off' beat; 4: step right, together, step left, together.) Make sure the children rehearse well so that they move together, exactly on the beat, and the performance looks polished and professional. Don't let them forget to smile a bit while they are concentrating on their moves – but big cheesy grins make it difficult to sing. When they can both sing and dance confidently, perform the song for an assembly.

Achievement

Can decode simple staff notation. Can sing in a gospel style. Can move in time to the beat. Can perform with style.

SONG SHEET 25

I'm Gonna Sing

Traditional spiritual
Arranged by George Odam

2. I'm gonna shout when the spirit says 'shout!'
    and obey the spirit of the Lord.

3. I'm gonna clap when the spirit says 'clap!'
    and obey the spirit of the Lord.

4. I'm gonna dance when the spirit says 'dance!'
    and obey the spirit of the Lord.

Deciphering the Code

Look at the music for 'I'm Gonna Sing'. Reading music is all about decoding a musical message, and much of the code is very easy to decipher.

First, look at the number 4 perched on top of a note at the beginning of the song. This gives the **metre** of the song, and in this case it tells us that the song has a 4-beat pattern to each bar.

A **bar** is the vertical line that separates each 4-beat pattern. It makes it much easier to read the music notes if they are neatly divided into equal sections.

A **note** is a symbol for a musical sound. Look at the five lines on which the notes are placed. This is called a **stave**, and notes are placed higher or lower on the stave to represent higher or lower sounds. Notice how the song moves along the lines from left to right, just as words do when we are reading.

If you look carefully, you will see that there are several different kinds of note. Some are white, some are black, some have hooks on their stems, and some are joined in pairs. These differences tell us how long or short the sounds are.

The signs at the end of each line, which look like number 7s, are called **rests**. They tell us to keep silent at those points.

ABOUT CHAPTER 6

Singing expressively

This chapter looks at the effect that tempo, dynamics and the accompaniment have on the mood of a song, and it suggests ways in which movement can be used to illustrate and enhance the mood and character of a song.

It briefly explains the similarities and the differences between the format of an opera, an oratorio and a musical and provides opportunities for listening to, and for recognising, the expressiveness and mood conveyed by a singer when singing and portraying a particular character.

The singing stance and posture is revisited with further guidance on singing loudly without having to use a shouting (belt) voice. Attention is given to understanding and performing written dynamics.

Help is given to address the pronunciation and articulation difficulties that occur when singing words that begin with a vowel.

Lesson	Focus
When You Live in a Lighthouse	Understanding the effect on mood of tempo and dynamics.
	Singing and observing expression marks.
	Singing consonants to enhance the expressive quality of a song.
Red Train	Creating a vocal soundscape.
	Listening for changes in the mood of a song.
	Changing the tempo and mood of a song.
	Adding movement to a song.
Singing actors	Understanding some differences between opera, oratorio and musical.
	Recognising that character can be expressed in singing.
King Richard's Song	Singing with the correct posture.
	Learning to sing loudly without shouting.

Singing expressively

When You Live in a Lighthouse

Focus

Understanding the effect on mood of tempo and dynamics. Singing and observing expression marks. Singing consonants to enhance the expressive quality of a song.

Resources

CD 3 tracks 1, 2; song sheet 27.

About the song

A specially composed children's song.

Activities

Tempo, dynamics and mood

Explain that when singing a song, the tempo and dynamics play a vital part in creating the mood of the song. For example, most lullabies are sung quietly and at a gentle, rocking pace: sing a lullaby too loudly or rock too fast and you will wake the baby.

Expressive warm-up

Play track 1. Both phrases have the same words, but one is sung in a manner to match the mood of the words and the other is sung inappropriately. Ask the children which phrase was sung most appropriately, at the right tempo (speed) (*the first phrase*). Discuss the effect of singing calm words to jolly music. (*There will be many answers, but the most important point is that the singer cannot communicate with the listener because neither party can understand what the song is about.*) Play track 1 again and ask the same questions, but this time focus on dynamics (loud and quiet).

Hearing the different dynamics

Use the song sheet with the class and discuss the meaning of the expression marks, written above the music (see Glossary on page 93). Play the song (track 2) and ask the children to listen specifically for the expression in the song. Which expressive element did they hear most clearly? What effect does the rallentando have on the last verse? (*It tells the listener that the song is about to end.*) How does the accompaniment help the mood of the song? (*It has a gentle rocking rhythm and sound effects.*)

Singing with expression

Encourage the children to practise the song, singing with track 2, until they know it by heart. Ask them to sing quietly while they are learning the song, so they will be able to hear themselves and their neighbours: this will help them to sing in tune. When they are confident, ask them to sing the song observing all the expression marks. Ask them to put a little emphasis on 'live', 'light', 'how' and 'be'. They should make sure the 'll's are pronounced in 'gull', and be careful when singing the following words as they all have inherent pronunciation difficulties. Leave a small gap between 'back' and 'yard': do not sing 'ba-ck-i-ard'. Leave a small gap between 'front' and 'yard': do not sing 'fronn-t-i-ard'. Lightly articulate the 'd' of wind and leave a small gap between 'wind' and 'and': do not sing 'winn-dand'. Lightly articulate the 't' and emphasise the 'h' in the word lighthouse: do not sing 'ligh-touse'.

Achievement

Can understand and relate tempo and dynamics to the mood of the song. Can sing, following given expression marks. Can sing consonants to enhance the expressive quality of a song.

SONG SHEET 27

When You Live in a Lighthouse

Words and music by Carmino Ravosa

1. The sea is your front yard, your back yard, your side. Your friends are the sea-gulls, the wind and the tide. When you live in a light-house, that's how it must be. When you live in a light-house by the side of the sea.

2. The sea is your window, your porch and your door.
You talk to the sea, to the waves, to the roar.

Singing expressively

Red Train

Focus

Creating a vocal soundscape. Listening for changes in the mood of a song. Changing the tempo and mood of a song. Adding movement to a song.

Resources

CD 3 track 3; song sheet 28.

About the song

This song is written by an Australian children's singer/songwriter.

Activities

Train soundscape

Talk about the train sounds that you can hear if you stand on the platform of a London underground station:

- the faint rumbling of the train in the distance before it comes into the station
- the increasing noise of the train as it approaches
- the breaks squealing as the train stops
- a voice over the loud speaker saying 'Mind the gap!'
- the dit, dit, dit, dit noise to signal the closing of the doors
- the train pulling out of the station with a loud grumbling noise
- the grumbling noise fading away as the train goes through the tunnel and out of sight.

There are several changes of mood in that sequence of sounds. Ask the children to create some vocal sounds to closely imitate the train sounds. They should use the full range of their voices and their imagination.

Listen for mood changes

Play the song on track 3. Discuss what makes the first and last sections of the song sound like a moving train. (*The continuous rumbling accompaniment imitates the train wheels going around.*) If your CD player has a balance control, use it to fade out the vocals so the children can hear the rumbling accompaniment. Play the song again and tell the children to listen for a change of mood in the middle section. (*The rumbling sound is no longer continuous, the melody is not as lively and bright, and the feeling is of worried passengers pushing to catch the next train.*)

Changing the speed and the mood

Let the children sing the song with the recording, and when they know it well ask them to sing it unaccompanied. (Try to sing songs unaccompanied as much as possible as it helps both you and the children to hear exactly what is being sung.) Set a faster tempo for the song and sing the first and last sections at the new speed. Ask the children how it alters the mood of the song. (*There will be several different answers, but the main reason is that the train feels as if it is going faster.*)

Added movement to enhance the mood

Ask the children to work in pairs and invent some movements to enhance the performance of the song. The movements should be simple and not detract from the song itself.

Achievement

Can contribute, with imagination, to a vocal soundscape. Can hear changes in the mood of a song. Can recognise how a musical mood can be changed. Can invent movement to enhance the performance of a song.

SONG SHEET 28

Red Train

Words and music by Peter Combe

Red train ___ un - der - ground, Grumb - ling ___ its rumb - ling sound, Red train ___ un - der - ground, In Lon - don town, Rush - ing ___ a - round, Up - stairs ___ and down, Push through ___ the gate, Push don't ___ be late.

Singing Actors

Focus

Understanding some differences between opera, oratorio and musical. Recognising that character can be expressed in singing.

Resources

CD 3 tracks 4, 5, 6

About the music

Opera: *The Magic Flute* by Wolfgang Amadeus Mozart. Soprano aria.

Oratorio: *Messiah* by George Frederick Handel. Bass aria.

Musical: *Oliver!* by Lionel Bart. Baritone song.

Activities

This lesson looks at extracts from three very different works that have been composed for the voice: the opera, oratorio and the musical.

Play each extract to the children – tracks 4 (opera), 5 (oratorio) and 6 (musical) – and enter into a general discussion about the different styles of singing. Explain that all three genres have solo singers and a chorus. Opera and oratorio use classically trained voices, usually without microphones, whereas musicals are more popular in style. Operas and musicals are acted on stage, like plays, with costumes, scenery and so on, while oratorios are usually sung 'concert style', with no action. Oratorios and many operas have a kind of 'sung speech' (recitative) between the main songs (arias), whereas many musicals – and some operas – have spoken dialogue between the songs. In more modern works, this distinction is becoming less and less obvious. Oratorios are based on religious (usually Biblical) stories.

Now ask the children to listen more carefully to the three extracts and to imagine the type of characters that are singing. Ask them to give reasons for their ideas and conclusions. After they have discussed their ideas, tell them what the composers had in mind when they were writing the soprano aria, the bass solo and chorus and the song for the musical.

Magic Flute. The Queen of the Night's aria

The Queen of the Night is a beautiful but evil enchantress. She sings an aria which is fast and highly decorated and famous for its high notes (high F, three octaves above middle C) and which befits a Queen whatever her persuasion! This type of singer is referred to as a 'Coloratura Soprano'. Do they think the singer conveys the character and her feelings well? If so, why?

Messiah. 'Why do the Nations'

The text is from the Bible, Psalm 2. ('Why do the nations so furiously rage together: Why do people imagine a vain thing?') The singing is very expressive: listen particularly for the words 'rage' and 'imagine'. How does the orchestral accompaniment set the mood? (*Fast, loud, insistent sounds*)

Oliver! 'I'm Reviewing the Situation'

This song is sung by Fagin, who is the leader of a gang of young criminals. In Dickens' book, Fagin is crafty and evil and is eventually tried and hung for his crimes. However, in the musical of Dickens' novel, he is portrayed as an impish, humorous character who evades the law and sings about his options for a future life. Do they think the singer conveys the character and his feelings? If so, why?

Achievement

Can understand and appreciate some main differences between opera, oratorio and musicals. Can recognise and discuss the expression of character in singing.

King Richard's Song

Focus

Singing with the correct posture. Learning to sing loudly without shouting.

Resources

CD 3 tracks 7, 8, 9; song sheet 29.

About the song

The music for this song was written by King Richard I of England (the 'Lionheart': 1157–1199) who was a keen musician. Singing and composing songs and poems was very fashionable when he was king. The original words were in French, because Richard couldn't speak English.

Activities

Identifying the character and mood

Play track 7 and ask the class to listen to the strong, rough and slightly nasal singing quality. (Use the balance control to isolate and to hear the vocals more clearly.) Explain that this song would have been sung to a street crowd, or to a theatre audience, by travelling musicians and poets known as Troubadors. People wouldn't stand politely and listen, so the Troubadors' singing had to be strong and clear to hold the crowd's attention. Ask the children to say the words through, imitating the 'medieval' accent. When the lyrics are secure, encourage the children to sing the song with the recording.

First Troubadors' performance

Divide the class into two groups – the crowd and the Troubadors. Sit the two groups on the floor and ask the Troubadors to sing loudly to the crowd imitating the slightly raucous nasal tone and the rumbustious style of the recording. Let the groups swap roles and repeat the exercise, then discuss the performances. Can they be improved, and if so, how? Because the singers were sitting down, it is likely that the singing lacked vigour and energy. It is possible that strong singing was taking place but probably by using a 'shouting' voice. Play track 8, **King Richard's Song** sung in a shouting voice. Would people be happy to listen to that type of singing for any length of time? Explain that to sing in that manner is tiring for the singer *and* the listener, and puts a heavy strain on the voice. Play track 9 to demonstrate good-quality loud singing.

Revising stance and posture

Look at the section on posture in 'All about singing' at the front of the book. Remind the children to take enough breath into the bottom of their lungs to last to the end of each line and to use their abdominal muscles to push the air energetically out of their lungs (see section on breathing in 'All about singing'). They should look at you, sing loudly with vigour and energy, but not shout. A slight emphasis on the first beat of every bar will give the song shape and a more musical feel.

Improved Troubadors' performance

Ask each group (now standing) to sing to the other again, and discuss how and why the quality of the singing has changed and, hopefully, improved. (*Standing in the correct stance always improves singing as it allows the diaphragm and 'tummy' muscles to work freely and the space in the lungs to be maximised – not squashed up as often happens when the children are sitting.*)

Achievement

Can stand correctly and sing maintaining the correct posture. Can sing loudly without shouting.

King Richard's Song

Richard Coeur de Lion
arrangement by George Odam

1. Rich - ard of Eng - land our Li - on - heart - ed king.

5. *Fine*
Now your re - turn to our fair land we sing.

9. Lift up your voic - es for Eng - land re - joi - ces.

13. *D.C. al Fine*
Free - dom from a ty - rant you bring!

ABOUT CHAPTER 7

Listening for singing

This chapter focuses on developing detailed listening, aural memory and inner hearing. Children need to be able to hear, in their head, what they want to sing before they actually sing it; this skill is essential for the accurate pitching of notes. Finding the correct pitches and creating melodies is often quite difficult without reference to a keyboard or tuned percussion instrument in the first instance, so there are some activities which suggest using instruments before memorising and transferring the melodies to the voice.

Opportunities are also provided for children to be able to 'feel' the steady beat in their head by creating short vocal and clapping patterns to fit into a predetermined number of beats.

The game of vocal copy cats is used in several disguises to help develop the aural memory, with rhythmic and vocal ostinato patterns being included in these games.

Work on 'vocal sound' conversations leads to writing and reading graphic scores.

There are activities to improve the techniques of rolling the letter 'r', humming with a buzz, stretching the vocal range, chanting and singing tongue twisters and singing with a swing.

Rounds and two-part songs are included as well as some solo work.

Lesson	Focus
Jazzstep	Listening to music with an awareness of the expressive use of pitch.
At the Hop (1)	Playing 'copy cat' with melodic phrases taken from a song.
	Chanting in canon.
	Singing in a 'pop' style.
	Moving or dancing in the rock 'n' roll style.
The Caravan	Identifying ostinato patterns.
	Singing ostinato patterns.
	Rolling the letter 'r'.
	Working at diction.
At the Hop (2)	Putting vocal and rhythmic patterns in a space.
	Singing and improvising simultaneously.
Shadow Song	Humming with a buzz.
	Paying attention to dynamics.
	Singing and clapping rhythm patterns.

Lesson	Focus	
Migildi Magildi	Working on words.	
	Singing a solo.	
	Inventing a 'vocal' conversation.	
	Writing a graphic score.	
Everybody	Singing and moving in the style of the song.	
Loves Saturday	Singing in a round.	
Night (2)	Playing by ear.	
High and Low	Improving high notes.	
	Improving diction.	
	Reading from a graphic score.	
	Evaluating and analysing their own vocal sounds.	

Chapter 7

Listening for singing

Lesson 1

Jazzstep

Focus

Listening to music with an awareness of the expressive use of pitch.

Resources

CD 3 tracks 10, 11, 12.

About the jazz piece

Courtney Pine ((1964–) soprano saxophone, bass and keyboard) merges different vibes together through the powers of jazz (improvised) and technology (computers). He is able to produce sound that is both old and new at the same time.

Activities

Wailing and screeching

Play track 10. Ask for a group of two or three volunteers to come up to the front and copy the singer's wailing sound. Encourage them to make the same 'unpleasant' sound that the singer made. Praise them for copying the sound of the singer so well; ask them how it felt to make such a sound. (*Answers might be: hurt their throat; felt silly; difficult.*) Ask the class how it felt to have to listen. (*Answers could be: frightened; hurts my ears; edgy, unpleasant.*) Explain that sort of tonal quality is rarely used in singing – only for special effects.

Beautiful high notes

Play track 11 and ask the class to have a go at copying the second sound. Tell them to sing only as high as they can comfortably manage and not to force their voices. How does it makes them feel to sing pleasant high notes? (*Happy, alive, expecting something, amazed.*) Ask them to do it again, but this time to rest their hand on their Adam's Apple and to notice how it moves up towards the chin as the higher pitches are sung.

The quality of high sounds

Tell the class that high sounds can be very expressive for good and for bad. A scream can mean that someone is either happy or sad. High notes in a piece of music or a song can be used to signify a very important point in that piece – often the climax of the whole piece.

Long, high and quiet

Play Jazzstep (track 12) and ask the children to listen out for the long high saxophone note. Ask them to describe the long note and to explain how that sound makes them feel. (*Answers could be: amazed; very clever to play such a high note; thin sound; they wondered how long the note was going on for.*)

Achievement

Can recognise the impact of high notes. Can describe their feelings when high notes are played or sung. Can recognise the movement of the epiglottis (Adam's Apple) in relation to pitch.

Lesson 2

At the Hop

Focus

Playing 'copy cat' with melodic phrases taken from a song. Chanting in canon. Singing in a 'pop' style. Moving or dancing in the rock'n'roll style.

Resources

CD 3 tracks 13, 14, 15; song sheets 30, 31.

About the song

This song has its roots in the blues and was made popular in the late 1950s. Rock'n'roll music, with its associated dance, was a teenage sensation, reflecting the increased independence of the young, and it is still popular today.

Activities

Copy cats

The children sit in a circle. Play the first four-note melody on track 13, then use the pause button to stop the recording and ask a volunteer to copy (sing) the four notes. Play the second short melody and ask for another volunteer, and so on. Each melody is played twice on track 13 to help the children remember it, and you should encourage every child to have a go at copying the phrases. (Each phrase is marked on the song sheet).

Canonic hop

(See Glossary for 'canon'.) Sit the children in a circle and ask them to chant the song words slowly and rhythmically until they can say them easily. Play track 14 and focus their listening by asking them to identify when the second part comes in. (*At the end of the second bar, after 'even stroll'.*) Divide the class into two and practise, with track 14, chanting the verse of the song in canon. For the refrain, half the class chant 'Let's go to the hop' and the others chant 'Oh baby'. Everyone chants the last line together, copying the dynamics on the recording. If you have a balance control you can use it to remove the vocals from track 15 so the class can chant with recorded backing.

Singing the song

Play the song again (track 15) and ask the children to listen to the 'pop' singing style. This is energetic, robust singing with a rhythmically 'relaxed' style. Careful attention has to be given to ensure a good ensemble. (Watch out: the '–by' of the third 'Oh baby' is sung on a different note from all the others.) Do not allow the children to use a shouting voice.

Moving

Ask the class to think up some simple movements for the chorus (*e.g. finger clicking, alternate shoulders forward*). A small group could invent some different movement for the 'Oh baby' phrases. If you or any of the children know the rock'n'roll steps, they could be performed by some children while the rest sing.

Achievement

Can copy a given rhythmic or melodic pattern. Can sing in rock'n'roll style. Can dance or add movement in rock'n'roll style.

SONG SHEET 30

At the Hop

Words and music by Arthur Singer,
John Medora and David White

Verse Phrase 1 Phrase 2

1. Well you can rock it, you can roll it, do the stomp and e - ven stroll it at the hop.

3

When the rec - ord starts a - spin - nin' you ca - lyp - so when you chick - en at the hop.

4

Do the dance sen - sa - tion that is sweep - in' the na - tion at the hop.

SONG SHEET 31

At the Hop (continued)

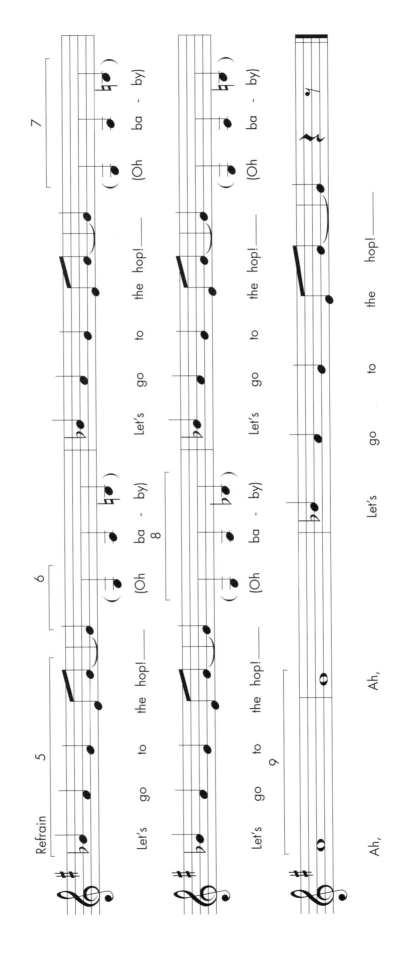

Refrain

Let's go to the hop! — (Oh ba - by)

Let's go to the hop! — (Oh ba - by)

Let's go to the hop! — (Oh ba - by)

Let's go to the hop! — (Oh ba - by)

Let's go to the hop! —

Ah, Let's go to the hop! —

Ah,

2. Well you can swing it, you can groove it,
You can really start to move it at the hop.
Where the jumpin' is the smoothest
And the music is the coolest at the hop.
All the cats and chicks will go to get their kicks at the hop.

Chapter 7

Listening for singing

Lesson 3

The Caravan

Focus

Identifying ostinato patterns. Singing ostinato patterns. Rolling the letter 'r'. Working at diction.

Resources

CD 3 tracks 16–20; song sheets 32, 33.

About the song

This is a folk song from Syria, in two vocal parts. The wind instrument in the accompaniment is called a *shehnai* and is often associated with snake charming.

Activities

Spot the 'ostinato'

This song has two vocal parts. Listen to track 16 to hear only the lower vocal part with the instrumental backing. Ask the class how many times the short vocal melody is repeated. (*4 times*.) Explain that when a short melody or rhythm is repeated over and over again, it is known as an ostinato. Track 17 has both vocal parts: if your CD player has a balance control you can remove the instrumental backing in order to hear them more clearly. Ask the children to listen to how the two vocal parts fit together.

Rolling 'r's

Play track 18 and ask the children to copy the singer. There are bound to be those who cannot roll their 'r's, but telling them to continually breathe out and to flip the 'r' very lightly with their tongue, like the beginning of a soft purr, may help. Also, it is easier if the preceding consonant is very short and light. This will improve with practice. Ask the class to think of other consonants to use before the rolled 'r' sound.

Sing the ostinato

If you have a balance control, use it with track 19 to teach the two different vocal parts of the song, reminding the class to make sure the 'tr' of 'tramp' has a short, light 't' and a soft rolled 'r'. Only when both vocal parts are really secure and can be sung unaccompanied, should you attempt to put them together.

Singing Animal Ostinati

Play track 20 and ask the children to guess which line of music represents an animal, which an insect, which a bird and which a fish. (*1 bird; 2 bee; 3 fish; 4 elephant*.) Play the **Animal Ostinati** again and ask the children to sing each line to 'la'. When they know the notes well ask them to put in the animal words. (To sing 'tweet, tweet' repeatedly, move only the lower lip; try not to say 'too-weet' as that makes it harder to say. It is also tricky to sing on a 'zz'; the secret is to keep breathing out. For 'trump' see 'tramp', above.) Help the children to learn all four parts from memory, and then ask them to combine two, three or all four parts together.

Achievement

Can identify an ostinato pattern. Can sing an ostinato pattern. Can roll their 'r's. Can improve their diction.

The Caravan

Folk song from Syria

SONG SHEET 33

Animal Ostinati

Alison Ley

Bird — Tweet tweet tweet etc.

Bee — Bz Zz Zz Zz Zz Zz Zz Bz Zz Zz Zz Zz etc.

Fish — Mwah Mwah Mwah Mwah etc.

Elephant — Trump Trump trump trump trump trump trump etc.

Sounds of Singing Y3–4/P4–5 © Alison Ley, Nelson Thornes Ltd, 2003

Listening for singing

Lesson 4

At the Hop (2)

Focus

Putting vocal and rhythmic patterns in a space. Singing and improving simultaneously.

Resources

CD 3 tracks 15, 21; song sheets 30, 31.

About the song

This song has its roots in the blues and was made popular in the late 1950s. Rock'n'roll music, with its associated dance, was a teenage sensation, reflecting the increased independence of the young, and it is still popular today.

Activities

Memorising short melodic patterns

Play track 21 and ask the class to perform a 'tap–pat–pat–pat' pattern (tapping two fingers in the palm of the hand and then patting the knees) throughout, in time to the steady beat. Do this activity until they can keep a uniform steady beat and until they are very familiar with the short melodic patterns.

Sing in the space

Play track 21 again and ask the children to tap/pat the steady beat only when the piano is heard. Ask them to sing, during the eight silent beats (the space), exactly what the singer has just sung. Pay attention to the intonation (the accurate pitching of the notes). Now try doing the same thing again, but this time challenge the children to sing their own improvised eight-beat melodic pattern as an answering phrase. For some children, this may be too difficult at first, so either ask them to sing a four beat melodic pattern and repeat it, or clap an improvised eight-beat rhythmic pattern instead.

Hop space

Play track 15, **At the Hop**, and ask the children to count the number of beats in the vocally silent space at the end of each line. (*There are seven before the voice comes in again, but it is permissible to tap the full eight beats.*) Tell the children that that space is usually filled with an instrumental improvisation. Ask them to invent and clap either a short rhythmic pattern or to play a short melodic pattern to fill the space. When they can do this with ease, the class should sing the song and individuals clap or sing their pattern in the space.

Achievement

Can copy a short vocal pattern. Can improvise a melodic or rhythmic four- or eight-beat pattern. Can invent and clap an eight-beat rhythm whilst singing a song.

Chapter 7

Listening for singing

Lesson 5

Shadow Song

Focus

Humming with a buzz. Paying attention to dynamics. Singing and clapping rhythm patterns.

Resources

CD 3 tracks 22, 23; song sheet 34.

About the song

A song to inspire the children's imagination.

Activities

Learning the melody.

Play the warm-up exercises on track 22 and ask the children to copy them exactly – especially the dynamics. Split the class in half and let each half perform the exercises to the other half. Ask them to try and remember the quality of the sound they hear.

Humming a buzz

The best humming has to be practised. Tell the children to put the tip of their little finger between their teeth, and to touch the underside of their finger with the tip of their tongue. Now they should take their finger out, keep their teeth and the tongue where they are, and lay the top lip lightly on the lower lip. Now hum the warm-up exercises again, and they will probably feel their lips tingling (vibrating). The class should hear the difference in the quality of the sound from the earlier humming. Practise until they can feel their lips buzzing. It sometimes helps to get the buzz effect by humming quite loudly, still keeping the lips touching lightly. Humming helps a singer to feel the correct singing 'place': i.e. 'forward' and not back in the throat. Singing from the back of the throat does not make a pleasant sound.

Humming and singing the song

Invite the class to learn the melody of **Shadow Song** by humming along with track 23. Take careful note of the dynamics marked on the song sheet. Remind the children not to squeeze their lips together. When they know the melody well, add the words. Remind them to keep the same gentle sound and to feel the same sensation of singing 'forward' (but without the buzzing) as they did when they were humming.

Singing and clapping shadow rhythms

Children sit in a circle. Play the song and talk about how shadows can be long (*evening shadows*), short (*midday shadows*), crisp (*in full sun*), blurred (*in weak sunshine*). Ask the children to choose which type of shadow they would like to be. Establish a steady pulse in metre of 4, and let them practise singing a long or a short pattern, a very rhythmic or a freer pattern. When they have rehearsed their own individual pattern ask each child in turn to sing their shadow pattern whilst the rest of the class pat the steady pulse.

Achievement

Can hum with a buzz to make a 'forward' sound. Can sing with appropriate dynamics. Can sing and/or clap a rhythm pattern to a steady beat.

Shadow Song

Joan K. Arnold

1. In the sun-shine, close to me, my sha-dow's at my feet.

In the gar-den, on the path, or walk-ing down the street.

I can dance or skip or run, my sha-dow's al-ways there.

Ev-en though I go quite fast, it fol-lows ev'-ry-where.

2. In the sunshine, close to me, my shadow's at my feet.
    In the garden, on the path, or walking down the street.
    As I pass the hours away and day draws into night
    The sun goes down, my shadow too just vanishes from sight.

Sounds of Singing Y3–4/P4–5 © Alison Ley, Nelson Thornes Ltd, 2003

Chapter 7

Listening for singing

Lesson 6

Migildi Magildi

Focus

Working on words. Singing a solo. Inventing a 'vocal' conversation. Writing a graphic score.

Resources

CD 3 tracks 24, 25, 26, 27; song sheet 35; paper and pencil.

About the song

A Welsh folk song in call and response style. It is about a blacksmith and uses onomatopoeic nonsense words for the response. The typical hammer blow of a smith is a hard blow followed by two bouncing or glancing blows, making the 'migildi' rhythm.

Activities

Facial workout

Ask the children to imagine that they are chewing a huge sticky toffee, which has got stuck on their teeth so they have to use their tongues to work it loose. Now imagine they have just eaten a very sugary doughnut and they have to stick their tongues out as far as they can in order to lick the sugar off from around the outside of their mouth. Now imagine they have put lip balm on their lips and have to rub them together to make the balm really soak in. These facial exercises warm up and loosen up the muscles, lips and tongue in preparation for work on good articulation.

Tongue twisters

Play the **Many Men** warm-up on track 24. Ask the class to copy it, but at a far slower speed than the recording. Only increase the speed when the children can sing the exercise well. Do the same with tracks 25 and 26 (**Mix some Mince** and **Chop a Chip**).

Solos

Play the song on track 27 and ask the children to join in the response. If you have a balance control, use it to hear the words without the backing. Can the class hear how clearly and precisely the words are articulated and how they have a slight lilt? They should make their lips and tongue work overtime for the words 'migildi magildi'. Divide the class in half and ask one half to sing the call and the other half the response. Ask for volunteers to sing the call as a solo.

Vocal conversations

The children should work in pairs. Tell them they are about to have a 30-second conversation but without using any words. They can make any kind of vocal sound (squeaking, whispering, huffing and puffing, sighing, crying, whooping, laughing, squealing, tongue clicking, etc.) but the conversation must sound as if it has some sort of meaning. (Perhaps a parent telling a child to go to bed, but the child wants to watch some more TV. What is the outcome? Does the child scream and shout, or go quietly to bed when the parent promises to video the programme?) When the children have made up their own scenario and practised their conversation several times, ask them to write the sounds down on paper using signs, symbols and pictures. Allow them to perform their conversations to each other. Finally, swap the graphic scores so that each pair interprets and performs someone else's score.

Achievement

Can perform tongue twisters with clarity. Can perform a solo. Can invent a vocal conversation. Can write a graphic score.

Migildi Magildi

Welsh folk song
Words by J. P. Dobbs

1. What a fine and pleas-ant sight, Mi-gil-di ma-gil-di hi now now,

In the smith-y warm and bright, Mi-gil-di ma-gil-di hi now now,

From the an-vil sparks are glan-cing, Mi-gil-di ma-gil-di hi now now,

Un-der-neath the ham-mer dan-cing. Mi-gil-di ma-gil-di hi now now.

2.   What a fine and pleasant race, Migildi magildi hi now now,
For the warmest brightest place; Migildi magildi hi now now,
When outside the winds are blowing, Migildi magildi hi now now,
And inside the fire is glowing, Migildi magildi hi now now.

3.   What a fine and pleasant sound, Migildi magildi hi now now,
When the songs and tales go round, Migildi magildi hi now now,
Clang of hammer, blow of bellows, Migildi magildi hi now now,
In the comp'ny of good fellows, Migildi magildi hi now now.

Chapter 7

Listening for singing

Lesson 7

Everybody Loves Saturday Night (2)

Focus

Singing and moving in the style of the song. Singing in a round. Playing by ear.

Resources

CD 3 track 28; CD 2 track 31; song sheet 24.

About the song

This folk song from Ghana may be sung as a round. A round is a vocal 'perpetual' canon in which the voices sing the same melody but enter in turn.

Activities

Becoming familiar with the melody

Play CD 2 track 31 to familiarise the class with the melody. Now play CD 3 track 28 and talk about the difference between the two phrases. (*The first is sung straight whilst the second is sung with a swing. In the second phrase the melody also slides on the word 'night' and it has a more robust quality to the singing.*) Talk about the singing style and ask why this song has to be sung with a swing and in a more relaxed manner. (*To convey its character and identity.*) To give this song a truly African feel, ask the children to add some simple body swaying movements or finger clicks as they sing.

Singing the round

When the children know the words and the melody well, teach them to sing it as a two-part round, with the second part coming in as the first part begins the third line. Do not be tempted to sing this song as a four-part round until the two-part round is secure, rhythmic, in tune and from memory.

Playing by ear

Some children may like to work out how to play one or more of the four lines of the song on a pitched percussion instrument.

Achievement

Can sing and move in the style of the song. Can sing a round. Can play by ear.

High and Low

Focus

Improving high notes.
Improving diction. Reading
from a graphic score.
Evaluating and analysing their
own vocal sounds.

Resources

CD 3 track 29; song sheet 36.

About the song

This is a vocal piece written as
a graphic score.

Activities

Tape record the children's first attempts at any of the following activities.
Then record their final attempt and let them hear how much they have
improved.

Increasing the vocal range.

Chapter 1 looked at the expressive use of high notes. To improve the
children's vocal range, play the vocal piece on track 29, **High and Low**. Let
them listen to it several times and describe the different vocal sounds (not
the pitches). Now use the song sheet and ask them to follow the graphic
score as **High and Low** is played. You may prefer to draw the score on the
board or use the overhead projector so you can point to the music and
everyone can follow your pointer. Let the children practise some of the
sounds on a single note in the middle of their range. They should not force
their voices in any way.

Singing High and Low

Now see if the children can sing **High and Low**. Point from left to right
across the score giving the speed of the music, or count the numbers at the
top of the score – these show when the vocal sound changes. You do not
have to go at the same speed as the recording. Make sure the children do
not force their voices and do not let them sing any higher than is
comfortable to achieve a pleasant sound. Are the children happy with their
sounds? How can they improve their performance? As the pitches get higher
ask the children to gently drop their bottom jaw and not to point their chin
upwards – no exaggerated movement is necessary. Can they feel their throat
open up as they sing higher? It will take quite a while for everyone to make
progress, but this is a really good exercise to do at the beginning of a singing
session and regular workouts will gradually improve their sense of pitch and
their vocal range.

Inventing tongue twisters

Revisit the tongue twisters in chapter 7 lesson 6 (CD 3 tracks 24, 25, 26).
Ask the children to work in pairs and *say* the tongue twisters to each other.
Between them they should decide whether the words were clear or not.
There should only be one 's' sound and one 'm' sound in **Mix some mince**;
it is very difficult to pronounce both the 'x' and the 's' (mix some) and the
two 'm's (some mince). Could the 'p's be heard in **Chop a Chip**? Were they
going too fast? They should practise until they have improved on their first
rendition. Now ask the children to make up their own tongue twisters to the
same tune (Rossini's William Tell Overture).

Achievement

Can improve their vocal range. Can evaluate their own singing. Can decide
on ways to improve their singing. Can improve their diction. Can follow a
graphic score.

High and Low

High

Low

1 2 3 4 5 6 7 8 9 10

hah hah hah

We e e e e e e e e e e e e e e e e e e e e e e e e e e e e e e e e e e e e e e e e e e e e e e e e e e e e e e e e e e e e w o o o o o o o

o o o o o o o o o o o o o o o o o o o o o o o o o o o o o o o o o o o o o

m m m m m m m

m m m m

Brr
Brr
Brr
Brr
Brr
Brr
Brr

Bzz
Bzz
Bzz

z z z z z z z z z z z z z z z z z z z z

hah hah
hah

ah ah ah ah ah ah ah ah ah ah ah ah ah ah ah

Responding to structure

This chapter focuses on performing. It makes suggestions for improving presentation by creating, recording, rehearsing and performing detailed movements which will complement the mood and style of a song and which will also reflect some of its musical features.

It looks at recognising and responding to the off beat, at keeping pace with an increasing tempo and at unanimity of movement.

There is an opportunity to discover the mechanics of writing new lyrics to an established melody, and a chance to do some further work on singing simple two-part songs.

Lesson	Focus
Dayenu	Responding to the 'off' beat.
	Clapping with an increasing tempo.
	Singing in two parts.
	Performing to an audience.
Calypso	Recognising when it is appropriate to put new words to a song.
	Singing a two-part calypso.
	Interpreting choreographed movement.
	Inventing and recording movements.
	Performing and engaging an audience.
Floating in Space	Describing the mood of a song.
	Listening in detail for musical features.
	Creating movement to reflect the musical features.
	Performing, presenting and engaging an audience.
Summer Holiday	Singing and dancing in the style of the period.
Barges	Quiet, contemplative singing.
	Capturing the gentle mood with appropriate movement.
	Attending to movement unanimity.
	Singing a solo.

Chapter 8

Responding to structure

Lesson 1

Dayenu

Focus

Responding to the 'off' beat. Clapping with an increasing tempo. Singing in two parts. Performing to an audience.

Resources

CD 3 tracks 30, 31; song sheet 37.

About the song

This song is based on the story of how Moses led the Children of Israel out of Egypt, away from slavery under Pharaoh. 'Dayenu' means 'we are satisfied'. The traditional words meant that 'if God had only taken us out of Egypt and given us the *torah* (law), we would have been satisfied'.

Activities

Spot the speed

Play track 30. Ask the class what the most obvious musical feature of this song is. (*It increases in tempo during each refrain.*)

Responding to the 'off' beat

This song is in metre of 4 and has a very strong 2nd and 4th beat to each bar. These strong 'off' beats drive the music along. Play only the verse (marked on the song sheet). Ask the children to clap on the 'off' beats – i.e. beats 2 and 4. When they can do this, ask them to make up a simple movement (e.g. banging alternate heels to the floor or slapping alternate thighs) to replace the clapping.

Speedy clapping pattern

Play the refrain, and ask the children to think of a clapping pattern which they can perform on every beat of the bar – i.e. on all 4 beats. The integrated movement of the clap must be simple enough to carry out even though the tempo quickens. The children will be performing this as a 'choir' so the movement must also be visually acceptable to an audience; therefore, large movements would probably not be appropriate. For the sake of visual unanimity, care should be taken with the clapping so that everyone makes movements of the same size.

Performing to an audience

Use the recording to teach the children the song – either in unison or in two parts. If your CD player has a balance control, use it with track 31 to highlight one or other of the vocal parts. If you do ask the children to sing the song in two parts, make sure that both parts can be sung from memory before attempting to put them together. For presentation purposes, select some children to sing the song whilst others do the movement. To lengthen the performance, this song could be played through three times: the first time with the backing only, the second time moderately loud and with the vocals, the third time at a louder volume. The movements (clapping and stamping) could increase in volume with each rendition.

Achievement

Can clap on the 'off' beat. Can keep time with increasing tempo. Can sing in two parts. Can perform, can present and can engage an audience.

Dayenu

Israeli folk song

Verse

1. He will take us out of E - gypt, take His peo - ple out of E - gypt,
2. He has giv - en us the Tor - ah, giv - en us the ho - ly Tor - ah,

He will take us out of E - gypt. Day - e - nu.
He has giv - en us the Tor - ah,

Refrain

accelerando

Day, day - e - nu,—— Day, day - e - nu,——

Day, day - e - nu, Day - e - nu, day - e - nu, day - e - nu,

Day, day - e - nu,—— Day, day - e - nu,——

Day, day - e - nu, day - e - nu, day - e - nu!

Sounds of Singing Y3–4/P4–5 © Alison Ley, Nelson Thornes Ltd, 2003

Chapter 8

Responding to structure

Lesson 2

Calypso

Focus

Recognising when it is appropriate to put new words to a song. Singing a two-part calypso. Interpreting choreographed movement. Inventing and recording movements. Performing, presenting and engaging an audience.

Resources

CD 3 tracks 32, 33; song sheets 38, 39, 40.

About the song

This song is a calypso – a type of folk song from the Caribbean. Calypsos are usually about political or social topics, or about love. The song is often made up on the spot to celebrate an event.

Activities

Listening to the Calypsos

Play the children track 32 (New Year Calypso), then track 33 (Happy Birthday Calypso). What is the difference between the two versions? (*Different words, one version sung by a group of children and the other by a solo singer.*) Has the mood of the song changed or is it still the same? (*The same.*) Explain that providing the mood of the words fits the music, then different words can be used with the same music. This often occurs with music which has its roots in a folk tradition.

Learning both songs

Teach one version of the song. If your CD player has a balance control, you can use it to highlight the different vocal parts on track 32. Do not put both parts together until they can be sung independently and from memory. Pay attention to the breathing marks for the lower part: the first four bars are all sung in one breath. Once the singing is secure, use the balance control to remove the vocals from track 33 so the children can sing with the backing only.

Interpreting and inventing new choreography

Using the movement plan, help the class to work out the choreography. Some children may be able to work out the actions for themselves. When the class can perform the movement for the first four lines, ask them to make up some more actions for the refrain, notating them in words or symbols. Where the words of the song are the same, the movement could also be the same. (Recording movement is very wordy and quite a difficult process. Every detail has to be addressed if the movement is to be correctly interpreted. Keeping movements simple not only looks better, but is also easier to record.) Some children may like to invent different movements for the New Year version of this song. Once again, the words as well as the music will govern the character and mood of the movement.

Performing and presenting

Give a performance of this song on every birthday. Those children whose birthdays are in the holidays could have 'un-birthdays'! The success of any movement is the accuracy of the ensemble. The more the movements are practised the more the brain remembers which muscles to move, how much and for how long and the more pleasing the result.

Achievement

Can understand what is required before new words can be put to existing music. Can sing in two parts. Can interpret recorded movement. Can invent and record movement to fit the mood of a song. Can perform, can present and can engage an audience.

SONG SHEET 38

New Year Calypso

Shena Power

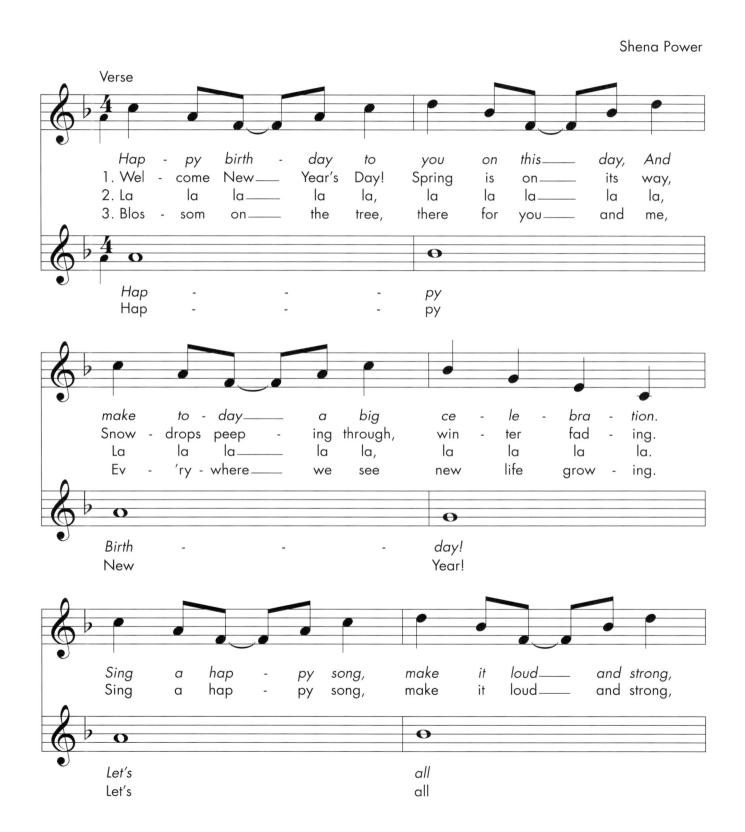

SONG SHEET 39

New Year Calypso (continued)

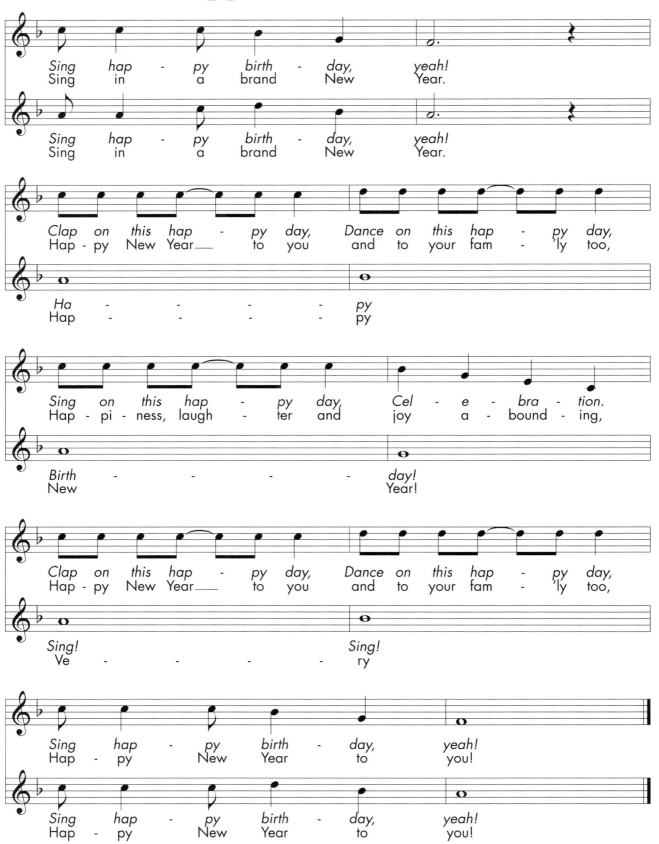

Sing hap - py birth - day, yeah!
Sing in a brand New Year.

Sing hap - py birth - day, yeah!
Sing in a brand New Year.

Clap on this hap - py day, Dance on this hap - py day,
Hap - py New Year___ to you and to your fam - 'ly too,

Ha - - - - - py
Hap - - - - - py

Sing on this hap - py day, Cel - e - bra - tion.
Hap - pi - ness, laugh - ter and joy a - bound - ing,

Birth - - - - day!
New Year!

Clap on this hap - py day, Dance on this hap - py day,
Hap - py New Year___ to you and to your fam - 'ly too,

Sing! Sing!
Ve - - - - ry

Sing hap - py birth - day, yeah!
Hap - py New Year to you!

Sing hap - py birth - day, yeah!
Hap - py New Year to you!

Happy Birthday Calypso

Words by Alison Ley

Happy birthday to you on this day and
Make today a big celebration.
Sing a happy song, make it loud and strong,
Sing happy birthday, yeah!

Clap on this happy day, dance on this happy day,
Sing on this happy day. Celebration!
Clap on this happy day, dance on this happy day,
Sing happy birthday, yeah!

Happy Birthday movement plan

Birthday person stands slightly to the front and on the right-hand side of the group.

Line 1

Legs: feet slightly apart – do not lock the knees.
Arms: raise right arm to shoulder level. Keep fingers together and point hand, palm upwards, in direction of birthday person. Move head to look at birthday person. Take one bar to reach that position and on the word 'you' in the second bar, lock elbow with a little jerk. Stay in that position until line 2.

Line 2

Legs: feet slightly apart – do not lock the knees.
Arms: look forward, raise both arms high (above head) in the air, and swing them first to the left, then right, then left, then right. Palms are facing forward, fingers spread.

Lines 3 and 4

Legs: keep left leg straight, loosely bend right knee, and bounce on left leg for beats 1 and 2. Transfer weight to right leg and do the same for beats 3 and 4. Continue this movement until the last bar.
Arms: bring arms down and bend at the elbow. Close hands in a loose fist. When the weight is on the left leg move right fist forward approximately 150 cm and gently bounce the fist in the air for beats 1 and 2. Alternate this movement by doing the same with the left fist for beats 3 and 4. Continue this movement until the last bar.

Last bar

Legs: on the word 'Yeah!' the weight should be on left leg and the knee should be locked. Bend right knee, lift heel high and rest on ball and toes of foot.
Arms: straighten both arms, keep fingers together, palms upwards and 'point' in direction of birthday person. Half-turn the body in the same direction and focus eyes on birthday person.

Chapter 8

Responding to structure

Lesson 3

Floating in Space

Focus

Describing the mood of a song. Listening in detail for musical features. Creating movement to reflect the musical features. Performing, presenting and engaging an audience.

Resources

CD 3 tracks 34, 35; song sheet 41.

About the song

A modern song capturing the mood and timelessness of space.

Activities

Describing the mood

Play track 34, the backing track of **Floating in Space**. Ask the children what the music makes them think about and ask them to describe the mood. (*All answers are likely to be valid.*) Now play the song with the words (track 35) so that they can hear what mood and atmosphere the composer intended to convey.

Listening for musical details

Play the instrumentals again (track 34) and ask the children to listen for the rhythm pattern that the drum plays throughout the piece. (*The pattern is one strike at the beginning on the first bar, followed by two quick strikes at the beginning of the second bar; this is repeated to the end of the piece.*) Play the song (track 35) and ask the class to listen to the circular melodic pattern which is heard throughout the piece. It is a four–note pattern:

1. Starting note
2. down one note
3. down another note
4. up one note
1. starting note
2. down one note
    etc.

Ask the children to put their hand up if they can identify where that circular melody pattern goes slightly higher in pitch before returning to the original pitch. (*The third line.*)

Space movement

Working with the whole class, talk about, and decide upon, some appropriate movement to create a dance for this song. The music has a very weak pulse and the movement should reflect this. There are three main musical features to listen out for and to respond to: the first is the quiet drum beat, the second the circular movement of the melodic pattern, and the third the slightly higher pitch of the third line. Attention must also be paid to the legato (smooth) playing of the melodic pattern and to the short, random 'space sounds' which interject the smooth melodic line. The class could be divided into different groups for the different musical features, or they could work as one large unit, or have solo roles for the 'space sounds'.

Performing and presenting

Listening and responding to the music in such detail is not easy, so experiment with many different ideas until the children are happy with their decisions and can be proud of their performance.

Achievement

Can talk about the mood of a song. Can identify musical features. Can invent movement to reflect mood and musical features. Can perform, can present, and can engage an audience.

SONG SHEET 41

Floating in Space

George Odam

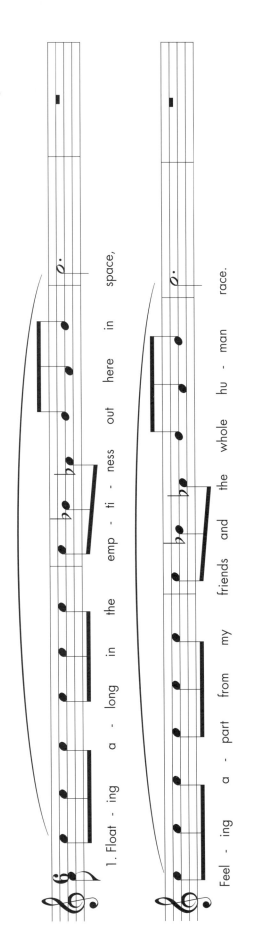
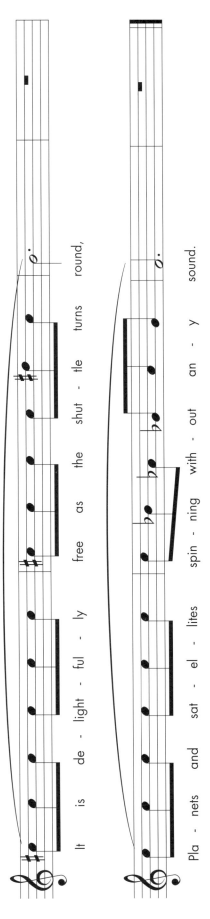

1. Float - ing a - long in the emp - ti - ness out here in space,
Feel - ing a - part from my friends and the whole hu - man race.
It is de - light - ful - ly free as the shut - tle turns round,
Pla - nets and sat - el - lites spin - ning with - out an - y sound.

2. They thought long ago that perfection in sound, to our ears,
Was made by the planets. They called it the song of the spheres.
And scientists tell us that sound can't be made without air,
But when I listen I know I can hear something there!

Chapter 8

Responding to structure

Lesson 4

Summer Holiday

Focus

Singing and dancing in the style of the period.

Resources

CD 3 track 36; song sheets 42, 43.

About the song

This song was a big hit in 1963 and comes from the light-hearted film of the same name. The film tells the story of how a garage mechanic (played by Cliff Richard) borrows a double-decker bus to go on holiday with a group of friends.

Activities

Drip-feed learning

Over the period of a week or two, play the song, track 36, to the children as they come into the classroom either first thing in the morning or at break times. It can also be played during classes when background music would be possible. In this way the children can learn both the words and the melody by the 'drip-feed' method. They can join in whenever they wish, humming the melody and adding the words as they pick them up.

Singing in a 'pop' style

Play the recording of the song, and ask the children to join in. Correct any wrong notes or words. Focus listening on the recorded singing. If your CD player has a balance control, use it to highlight the vocal track. Ask the class to listen for those words which have a 'pop' style pronunciation (*going, laughter, seen it in, everybody, wanted*). Practise saying those words and then sing the song again, but in this more relaxed vocal style. Encourage a light, bouncy feel to the singing.

About the style

The dances of the sixties are still performed today. The fast, energetic jive and the more acrobatic rock and roll dances were bought over from America and were particularly popular. If you know how to do these dances, or can obtain information from the library, dance clubs or the Internet, then it would be good to teach the children some of the more simple moves. It might be helpful to show some video clips from films of that era so that the children can compare today's disco and club dancing with the dancing of the sixties. Today's dancing has far less physical contact, with the dance being more of an individual expression rather than of two people responding to each other's moves.

Dancing in the style of the period

Ask the children to make up a simple sixties-style dance routine in pairs. Notice the song is in three sections, A B A. Create contrasting steps and moves for the 'B' section. The steps in the first 'A' section can be repeated in the second 'A' section. This is a fun song and the dancing needs to be imaginative and energetic but carefully controlled. Some children will find this free dancing quite difficult, so give them an alternative option of making up a hand jive to go with the song. Perform this dance as part of a whole school show.

Achievement

Can sing in the style of the period. Can dance in the style of the period. Can make up a hand jive to the steady beat.

Summer Holiday

Words and music by Bruce Welch and B. Bennett

SONG SHEET 43

Summer Holiday (continued)

Sounds of Singing Y3–4/P4–5 © Alison Ley, Nelson Thornes Ltd, 2003

Responding to structure

Lesson 5

Barges

Focus

Quiet, contemplative singing. Capturing the gentle mood with appropriate movement. Attending to movement unanimity. Singing a solo.

Resources

CD 3 track 37; song sheet 44.

About the song

This is a traditional song from The Netherlands. Because of the massive flood defences and subsequent land reclamation, much of The Netherlands is below sea level and there are many canals and rivers.

Activities

Matching the character of the song to the nature of the country

Play track 37 to the children. Ask them to describe the mood of the song (*peaceful and relaxed*). Tell them that the land in The Netherlands is very flat which gives a calm feeling when travelling through the countryside either on land or by boat.

Singing the song

Ask the children to imagine that they are sitting in a rocking chair looking out of their bedroom window, dreaming of sailing on one of the barges. Ask them to hum the song (see Chapter 7 lesson 5 for good humming technique) and to rock gently in the chair. Add the words when the melody is secure. Be careful to observe the breath marks. This could be difficult when sitting down, so remind the children about their breathing technique and about maintaining a good sitting posture.

Flowing arm movements

Ask the children to think of some arm movements that will go with the song. There should be no small or jerky movements, but large flowing movements using either one arm, or both arms together. Think of them as hand movements which you might use when telling the story of the song to a friend.

Performing

This would make a good contrasting song to perform with one of the more lively songs in this chapter. Pay careful attention to the movement unanimity, so that every child makes their movement the same size and duration as the rest of the group. Some children may like to sing the verse as a solo.

Achievement

Can sing quietly. Can make flowing arm movements in time with the rest of the group. Can sing a solo.

SONG SHEET 44

Barges

Traditional song from the Netherlands

Verse

1. Out of my win - dow, look - ing in the night,
Si - lent - ly flows the ri - ver to the sea,

I can see the bar - ges' flicker - ing light.
and the bar - ges too go si - lent - ly.

Refrain

Bar - ges, I would like to go with you.
Bar - ges, I would like to go with you.

I would like to sail the o - cean blue.
I would like to sail the o - cean blue.

2.   Out of my window, looking in the night,
I can see the barges' flickering light.
Starboard shines green and port is glowing red.
You can see the flickering far ahead.

90

Correlations

Singing is universal. While there may be differences of expression in the curriculum requirements and guidelines of different countries, in essence they are much the same and it is this common purpose that forms the basis of *Sounds of Singing*.

At the time of going to print, *Sounds of Singing* has been correlated to the following documents:

- National Curriculum 2000 (England)

- DfES/QCA Scheme of Work for Key Stages 1 and 2 Music (England)

- Music in the National Curriculum in Wales

- Expressive Arts 5–14 (Scotland)

These correlations may be viewed or downloaded free of charge from our Web site, www.nelsonthornes.com/soundsofsinging

The Northern Ireland Curriculum is under review at the time of writing. A correlation will be made as soon as possible.

All curriculum guidelines and requirements are subject to change, so please visit the Web site for updated correlation charts.

If you are have difficulty in accessing the Internet, hard copies of the correlations are available, also free of charge, from your Nelson Thornes representative or from our offices. Please telephone 01242 267280.

Sounds of Music

Sounds of Singing is a focused singing course, and has been designed so that it may be used to complement *Sounds of Music*. Many of the songs and listening extracts are common to both programmes, but all the lessons, activities and warm-ups in *Sounds of Singing* are new. If you wish to co-ordinate your use of the two schemes, the information below will help you to plan. You may also wish to use the *Repertoire in Sounds of Singing* in helping you to select content from *Sounds of Singing* to support your general music scheme of work.

Music also used in *Sounds of Music* Y3/P4

Asi Desh
Baba Yaga
Barges
Gest of Robyn Hode, A
I'm Gonna Sing
King Richard's Song
Rainy Day
Red Train
Shadow Song
Three Pirates

Music also used in *Sounds of Music* Y4/P5

At the Hop
Dance the Tango
Everybody loves Saturday Night
Floating in Space
Migildi Magildi
Mission Control
Oliver Cromwell
Piñata Song
Three Craw

Repertoire in Sounds of Singing Y3-4/P4-5

Songs and chants

	chapter	lesson	page	origin
African Chant	4	5	40	Traditional (Africa)
Asi Desh	1	3	8	Traditional (Punjab)
At the Hop	7	2	64–65	Rock'n'roll (USA)
Baba Yaga	5	2	46	Children's song (Britain)
Bamboo Tone, The	2	3	18	Traditional (China)
Barges	8	5	90	Traditional (Netherlands)
Battle of Badon Hill, The	2	1	13	Composed chant (Britain)
Caravan, The	7	3	67	Composed song
Dance the Tango	2	2	15–16	Children's song (Britain)
Dancing	3	2	24	Traditional (Slovakia)
Dayenu	8	1	79	Traditional (Israel)
Easter Bunny Hop, The	4	4	37–38	Children's song (Britain)
Edward J Fox	4	2	33	Children's song (Australia)
Everybody Loves Saturday Night	5	3	48	Traditional (Ghana)
	7	7	74	
Floating in Space	8	3	85	Children's song (Britain)
Gest of Robyn Hode, A	3	4	28	Traditional (Britain)
Happy Birthday Calypso	8	2	83	Children's calypso (Britain)
High and Low	7	8	76	Sound picture (Britain)
I'm Gonna Sing	5	4	50	Spiritual (USA)
King Richard's Song	6	4	59	Traditional (Britain)
Migildi Magildi	7	6	73	Traditional (Britain)
Mission Control	1	2	5–6	Children's song (USA)
Music's Mine	3	1	21–22	Children's song (Britain)
New Year Calypso	8	2	81–82	Children's calypso (Britain)
Oh Watch the Stars	1	1	3	Spiritual (USA)
Oliver Cromwell	5	1	44	Traditional (Britain)
Peter Piper	5	1	43	Traditional Chant (Britain)
Pimlico, Pamlico	1	3	7	Traditional Chant (Britain)
Piñata Song	3	3	26	Traditional (Mexico)
Rainy Day	4	1	31	Children's song (Britain)
Red Train	6	2	56	Children's song (Australia)
Shadow Song	7	5	71	Children's song (Britain)
Summer Holiday	8	4	87–88	Popular song (Britain)
Three Craw	4	3	35	Traditional (Britain)
Three Pirates	1	4	10	Traditional (Britain)
When You Live in a Lighthouse	6	1	54	Composed song (USA)

Vocal warm up exercises and listening extracts

	chapter	lesson	page	activity
Animal ostinati	7	3	68	Listening
Asi Desh (words only)	1	3	7	Warm up
Baba Yaga (spoken)	5	2	45	listening
Bongo knees A – E	3	2	23	Warm up
Canonic hop	7	2	63	Listening
Chop a chip	7	6	72	Warm up
Dargason, The	3	3	25	Listening
Deciphering the code	5	4	51	listening
Drone	2	3	17	Warm up
Find the Ring	3	3	25	Listening
Floating in Space (instrumental)	8	3	84	Listening
Follow the Horse banner	2	1	12	Warm up
Gest of Robyn Hode, A (doo-be-doo)	3	4	27	Warm up
High sound	7	1	62	Warm up
Hop patterns	7	2	63	Warm up
Humming	7	5	70	Warm up
Jazzstep, The (jazz)	7	1	62	Listening
King Richard's Song (not shouting)	6	4	58	Listening
King Richard's Song (shouting)	6	4	58	Listening
Lip gymnastics	1	3	7	Warm up
Loud snake sounds	1	1	2	Warm up
Magic Flute: The Queen of the Night (opera)	6	3	57	Listening
Many men	7	6	72	Warm up
Melodic patterns	7	4	69	Listening
Messiah: Why Do the Nations (oratorio)	6	3	57	Listening
Mix some mince	7	6	72	Warm up
Mood	6	1	53	Listening
Norwegian Mountain Dance	3	3	25	Listening
Oliver: Reviewing the Situation (musical)	6	3	57	Listening
Oo–ee sounds (pleasant)	1	2	4	Warm up
Oo–ee sounds (screechy)	1	2	4	Warm up
Pentatonic melodies	2	3	17	Listening
Peter Piper (other tunes)	5	1	42	Warm up
Peter Piper (tune 1)	5	1	42	Warm up
Pimlico Pamlico	1	3	7	Warm up
Quiet snake sounds	1	1	2	Warm up
Riding from Camelot	2	1	12	Warm up
Rockin' Rockets	3	3	25	Listening
Rolled 'r'	4	3	34	Warm up
	7	3	66	
Santa Claus laughs	1	4	9	Warm up
Saturday Night warm up	7	7	74	Warm up
Saxons marching	2	1	12	Warm up
Send out the skirmishers	2	1	12	Warm up
Singing nose (ning-nang)	4	5	39	Warm up
Singing nose (range)	4	5	39	Warm up
Singing nose (hum)	4	5	39	Warm up
Spoken Patterns 1–6	4	4	36	Warm up
Tango warm up	2	2	14	Warm up
Tapped Patterns 1–6	4	4	36	Warm up
Vowel warm up	4	3	34	Warm up
Wailing	7	1	62	Warm up

Glossary

ABA structure

a musical plan that has 3 sections: sections 1 and 3 are the same; section 2 is different

accelerando

getting faster

accent

a note, beat or pulse played or sung with more emphasis than those around it

accompaniment

music that supports the sound of the featured performer(s)

aria

italian word for 'song', in opera

articulation

clear enunciation of words

beat

a repeating pulse

call and response

a song in which two singers or groups sing alternately, the second responding to the call of the first

canon

one voice (or instrument) is imitated, note for note, by a second voice which enters later with the same melody, overlapping the first voice

chord

three or more different notes played together

chord sequence

a succession of chords. The chord sequence can be repeated and often provides the harmonic structure of a song

chorus

see 'refrain'

counter melody

a melody that weaves in and out of the main melody and is sung at the same time

crescendo

getting louder

cumulative

a song in which a new line is added to each successive verse

decrescendo

getting quieter

diminuendo

gradually getting quieter

diphthong

two vowel sounds pronounced as one syllable

drone

a continuous or repeated pitch or pitches

dynamics

the loudness and quietness of sound

ensemble

any combination of performers

the ensemble

the quality of a group performance, e.g. unanimity of attack, balance, tone

expression marks

symbols used to indicate how music should be performed: here are some common ones
p quietly (from Italian 'piano')
pp very quietly
mp moderately quiet (from Italian 'mezzo piano')
f loudly (from Italian 'forte')
ff very loudly
mf moderately loud (from Italian 'mezzo forte')
crescendo or *cresc.* or ‹ get louder
decrescendo or *decresc.* or › get quieter

rallentando or *rall.* get slower
accelerando or *accel.* get faster

glottal stop

a consonant sound produced by opening or shutting the glottis

glottis

the entrance to the windpipe

gospel song

a religious (Christian) song in a jazz or blues style, originating in the USA

graphic score

a representation of musical sounds using pictures, etc., rather than notation

improvisation

the art of making up and performing music, according to the inventive whim of the moment

intonation

the accurate pitching of musical notes

jazz

a style that grew out of the music of black Americans, then took many different substyles: ragtime, blues, Dixieland, cool jazz, swing bebop, rock, etc. It features solo improvisations over a set harmonic progression

leap

moving from one pitch to another, skipping the pitches in between, e.g. from D to G (see 'step')

legato

smoothly

metre

organisation of strong and weak beats (usually in 2s or 3s)

musical

popular stage show involving singing, drama, speech and dance, in costume

notation

the way in which music can be written down

note

symbols for sound in music (sometimes used as an alternative to 'pitch (1)')

note values

𝅝 = 4   𝅗𝅥 = 2   𝅘𝅥 = 1   𝅘𝅥𝅮 = ½   𝅘𝅥𝅯 = ¼

opera

dramatic show with singing, usually no speech, in costume

oratorio

religious (usually Christian) work for solo singers, chorus and orchestra

ostinato

a rhythm or melody pattern that is repeated many times, usually as an accompaniment

pentatonic

music based on a 5-pitch scale, e.g. CDEGA

percussion

instruments that are played by striking with beaters or by shaking

phrase

a musical 'sentence', sometimes marked by ⌒ over the notation

pitch (1)

a single musical sound (sometimes called 'note')

pitch (2)

the highness or lowness of sound

pitched percussion

percussion instruments which produce a specific pitch or pitches, e.g. chime bar

pulse

see 'beat'

rallentando

getting slower

recitative

'sung speech' in an opera or oratorio

refrain

the part of a song that repeats, with the same melody and words (see 'verse')

repetition

music that is the same, or almost the same, as music that was heard earlier

rest

silence between musical sounds

rest values

= 4   = 2   = 1   = 1/2   = 1/4

rhythm

the organisation of beat, no beat, long and short sounds, metre, tempo, etc.

round

a vocal perpetual canon, in which the voices sing the same melody but enter in turn

scat singing

jazz singing, improvised freely on syllables such as 'Doo-bi-doo-bi-doo'.

sequence

a phrase repeated but with a different starting pitch

spiritual

a religious song originating in the African American tradition

staccato

short and detached, indicated by a dot immediately above or below a note

staff

set of 5 lines on which music notes are placed to indicate pitch

staggered breathing

a technique used in choral singing. Each singer takes a breath at a different place during an extra-long phrase

stave

see staff

steady beat

regular pulse – the children clap 'in time'

step

moving from one pitch to the next, e.g. from B to C, or from F to F# (see leap)

structure

the overall plan of a piece of music

syncopation

placing a strong emphasis on the weak, or 'off' beat

tempo

the speed of the beat in music (fast, slow)

timbre

special quality (colour) of a sound – a flute has a different timbre from a violin

tuned percussion

see 'pitched percussion'

unaccompanied

see 'accompaniment'

unison

everyone singing or playing the same melody together

verse

the part of a song that repeats with the same melody but different words (see 'refrain')

vocals

singing

Acknowledgements

A Gest of Robyn Hode
from *Robin Hood* by George Odam © Chester Music Ltd.

Animal Ostinati
Composed by Alison Ley © Alison Ley

At the Hop
"At The Hop" composed by: John Medora/ Arthur Singer/David White © Conrad Music used by kind permission of Tristan Music Ltd

Baba Yaga
Words and music by George Odam © Chester Music Ltd

Bamboo Tone
Words by George Odam © Georgian Music DTP

Battle of Badon Hill
Words and music by George Odam © Georgian Music DTP

Dance the Tango
Words and music by Joan Arnold © Georgian Music DTP

Easter Bunny Hop
Words and music by George Odam © Georgian Music DTP

Edward J Fox
Words and music by Peter Combe © Bacalunga Music

Floating in Space
Words and music by George Odam © Georgian Music DTP

Happy Birthday Calypso
Words by Alison Ley © Alison Ley

King Richard's Song
from *Robin Hood* by George Odam © Chester Music Ltd

Migildi Magildi
Words by Jack P. B. Dobbs © Jack P. B. Dobbs

Mission Control
Words and music by Carmino Ravosa © Carmino Ravosa

Music's Mine
Words and music by George Odam © Georgian Music DTP

New Year Calypso
Words and music by Shena Power © Georgian Music DTP

Piñata Song
Words by Nick Curtis © Glenda Curtis

Rainy Day
Words and music by George Odam © Georgian Music DTP

Red Train
Words and music by Peter Combe © Bacalunga Music

Shadow Song
Words and music by Joan Arnold © Georgian Music DTP

Summer Holiday
Words and Music by Bruce Welch and Brian Bennett. © 1963 EMI Music Publishing Ltd trading as Elstree Music, London WC2H 0QY. Reproduced by permission of International Music Publications Ltd. All Rights Reserved.

When You Live In a Lighthouse
Words and music by Carmino Ravosa © Carmino Ravosa

Every effort has been made to trace all the copyright holders, but if any have been inadvertently overlooked the publishers will be pleased to make the necessary arrangements at the first opportunity.

528459

This item is to be returned on or before the last
due date stamped below .

Items can be renewed 3 times unseen.If a fourth
renewal is required the item must be brought
to the library.

1 2 JAN 2007		